FORT ADAMS

A HISTORY

John T. Duchesneau &
Kathleen Troost-Cramer

Published by The History Press
Charleston, SC 29403
www.historypress.net

Copyright © 2014 by John T. Duchesneau and Kathleen Troost-Cramer
All rights reserved

First published 2014

ISBN 978-1-5402-2459-0

Library of Congress CIP data applied for.

Notice: The information in this book is true and complete to the best of our knowledge. It is offered without guarantee on the part of the authors or The History Press. The authors and The History Press disclaim all liability in connection with the use of this book.

All rights reserved. No part of this book may be reproduced or transmitted in any form whatsoever without prior written permission from the publisher except in the case of brief quotations embodied in critical articles and reviews.

The authors dedicate this work to the men, women and children who served and worked, laughed and wept, lived and died at Fort Adams during its 150 years as an active base of the United States Army. You are not forgotten.

CONTENTS

Foreword, by Rick Nagele — 7
Acknowledgements — 11

PART I: BLOOD AND TREASURE, 1639–1824
The Revolution — 15
The Rock: Old Fort Adams — 20
"New" Fort Adams — 25

PART II: THE WARS OF THE NINETEENTH CENTURY
The Mexican-American War, 1845–1848 — 36
The Civil War — 43
The Spanish-American War and the End of the
  Nineteenth Century — 67

PART III: THE WARS TO END ALL WARS
The First World War — 74
The Second World War — 92
WACs, Workers and Wives: Women in the Life of Fort Adams — 100

PART IV: FALL AND RISE
Twilight Years — 112
Restoration: From 1965 to the Early Twenty-first Century — 117

Contents

Appendix A: Commanding Officers of Fort Adams — 127
Appendix B: Units Stationed at Fort Adams — 141
Appendix C: The Artillery of Fort Adams — 153
Notes — 175
Bibliography — 181
Index — 187
About the Authors — 191

FOREWORD

Our nation today is protected by projecting power well beyond our borders. Satellites, aircraft, ships, submarines and other military technologies ranging from drones to anti-virus software stand ready to protect us from threats. In earlier times, fortifications located at critical geographic points provided most of our protection.

The peninsula jutting into Narragansett Bay just southwest of Newport, Rhode Island's downtown has a long history as a home to fortifications. The current structure occupying the site, the largest and most complex coastal fortress in North America, was started in 1824 and occupied for well over a century. This fort's history is rich with important missions and colorful characters. Today, it is a National Historic Landmark and adventure/learning destination, offering guided and self-guided tours and a variety of team-building opportunities, as well as magnificent event space available for rent.

Fort Adams is significant primarily because of its role as a learning laboratory for builders of fortifications. In many ways, this fortress can be thought of as the NASA of its day. The builders experimented with critical construction elements and design features, tested, revised and recorded their findings. They then communicated their results to other construction teams throughout the United States. In a sense, Fort Adams is where America learned how to build sophisticated military systems.

Throughout much of its life, Fort Adams was "the good soldier, quietly doing his duty." Narragansett Bay is the only deep-water harbor

Foreword

between New York and Boston and therefore is an ideal place from which to launch an attack on either city. During the age of sail, it was also a safe harbor no matter what the wind direction—significant at the time. By its presence, the fort helped provide security to the entire U.S. Northeast by denying any enemy the use of Narragansett Bay.

During the Civil War, Confederate commerce raiders stalked the coast of New England and even attacked some smaller cities. Newport would have been easy prey to these enemy vessels if not for Fort Adams. Interestingly, the U.S. Naval Academy was relocated to Newport for the duration of the war. For a part of that time, the academy called Fort Adams home. During the summer of 2013, the National Geographic Channel program *Diggers* explored the fortress and found many artifacts from that period.

History has shown the Spanish navy to be ineffective during the Spanish-American War. At the time, however, U.S. citizens living in coastal communities were very afraid of being attacked by an overwhelming European power. Knowing that Fort Adams was "on duty" reassured many that their homes were safe.

During the Mexican-American War, World Wars I and II and into the Korean conflict, Fort Adams played a major role in preparing troops for overseas deployment. The fort also was responsible for command and control of the defenses of Narragansett Bay from Long Island, New York, to Buzzards Bay, Massachusetts. While many think that we were never attacked during these wars, German U-boats were sunk off New England's coast. In fact, the last German U-boat destroyed during World War II was sunk only a few miles away, off Block Island, Rhode Island.

It has been said that because the fortress was here, Narragansett Bay was never attacked. There may be some truth to this statement. Fort Adams did the job it was designed to do effectively yet without fanfare, evolving over time to meet the needs of a changing military.

The stories that authors John Duchesneau and Kathleen Troost-Cramer relate in this book begin even before the construction of the current fort. Enigmatic Irishmen, fraudulent counts, genuine French generals and U.S. Army engineering officers all play leading roles. Newport has a robust Irish community, which came here originally to build this mighty fortress. They stayed and, among other things, helped to build and then work in Newport's famous summer "cottages." Today, their descendants are among Newport's community leaders.

Foreword

Enjoy the book as you learn about the life and times of this magnificent place. Meet the famous, the sturdy, the competent and sometimes incompetent people who played important roles at Fort Adams and in life in Newport, Rhode Island. Perhaps you'll also gain some perspective on the history and growth of a great nation.

R. Nagele
Executive Director
Fort Adams Trust

ACKNOWLEDGEMENTS

JOHN T. DUCHESNEAU: It would be impossible to list all the people who have been a part of the great adventure I call my life and, thereby, made this book possible. I will admit that this list is fairly long, but as this book is my first, and as it was shaped by the many people who have influenced my life over the years, I don't feel it would be right to mention only a few. There are probably a few omissions, but I will try to avoid them.

First, I would like to thank my family. My father, for teaching me to love my country and to appreciate the importance of both learning and learning from history. My mother, who taught me about God's love, Christian values and also an appreciation of the beauty of nature. My brother Robert, for sharing his vast knowledge of diverse subjects with me and for teaching me that small pieces of information are as valuable as big ones.

Second, I want to thank all the people who have made Fort Adams a landmark tourist destination over the last twenty years. Frank Hale, for establishing the Fort Adams Trust and getting Fort Adams on the road to being restored. The Fort Adams Trust staff—Rick Nagele, Rob McCormack, Laurie Labrecque, Jack McCormack, Bill Goetzinger and Mike Pine—for making my dreams for Fort Adams a reality. Past staff members Tony Palermo, Mary Beth Smith and Eric Hertfelder, for all their hard work getting the fort's revitalization off the ground. Also, volunteers Chris Zeeman and Matthew "Doc" Perry, for their hard work in clearing brush and helping out at special events.

Third, I would like to thank the people who have helped me with my extensive research on Fort Adams. Bert Lippincott, the librarian of the Newport Historical Society, for his help with my research on various subjects and trying to answer my questions about obscure topics. Bolling W. Smith, one of the leading lights of the Coast Defense Study Group, for obtaining copies of hundreds of documents from the National Archives related to Fort Adams and sharing them with me. Dan Titus, for always being helpful and giving me access to his historical archives related to Newport and Fort Adams. Walter Schroeder, for writing his book *Defenses of Narragansett Bay in World War II*.

Fourth, I want to thank the organizations to which I belong that have given me an active social life and many valuable acquaintances—particularly the Artillery Company of Newport, for bringing history alive by connecting the past with the present. Also, the Sons of Union Veterans, the Sons of the Revolution, the Sons of the American Revolution, the Society of Colonial Wars, the Military Order of Foreign Wars, the Veterans of Foreign Wars and the American Legion. I would list the names of the people I am happy to know through these organizations, but it would be far too long.

Fifth, I would like to thank the many people I am privileged to call my friends. My dear friend Lyudmilla, for her love for and faith in me. My longtime best friend Lisa Carter, for her encouragement, conversation and kindness over the years. Larry McDonald, for his generosity and our long conversations on subjects of mutual interest. Laurie Shaw, for being a great friend as well as a wonderful person. Christopher Williams, for teaching me not to take myself, or life, too seriously. Brian "Doctor Love" Sullivan, for teaching me to see and appreciate the things others have overlooked. Chris Morse, for his compassion, insights and common-sense wisdom. Gregg Mierka, for his love of the "Boys in Blue" and for daring to dream larger than most people can imagine. Jim Feeney, for his honesty and insights into human nature. Scott Davey, for being an all-around cool guy who navigates life by his own compass. Eric Carpio, for his encouragement and for helping me keep it together when I needed to the most. Andy Howard, for having a big heart and seeing more in me than I knew was there. Kate Dimancescu, for showing me through her book *Forgotten Chapters: My Journey into the Past* that I should learn from the lives of my ancestors and honor their memory. Professor John Hattendorf, General Richard Valente and Colonel Theodore Gatchel, who, despite their high levels of professional achievement, saw some value in me and encouraged me to pursue my dreams. My many teachers, who gave me a love of knowledge and challenged me to realize my potential. Sue, Debbie, Reese, Kate, Natasha, Michelle, Lieva, Jamey and Mary, for serving me coffee and food for many years. The Table 3 Escadrille—Geoff, Tom, Rafael, John, Lexi, Maura and Carol—for some of the best conversation in history. The many soldiers with whom I have served in my military career, for their comradeship and their service to our country—often at great personal sacrifice. Tommy O'Hare, for being a real American hero, even though he would never think he was one. I also need to thank "Bubba" (who is too humble to wish to see his name in print), for all he has done for me over the years.

Finally, I thank my co-author, Kathleen Troost-Cramer; without her interest in Fort Adams, focus, organizational skills, common sense and ability to keep me focused, this book would probably never have been published.

KATHLEEN TROOST-CRAMER: I would like to echo John's thanks to the staff, employees and volunteers of the Fort Adams Trust, as well as to Dan Titus of Salve Regina University, and to add the following. Eternal gratitude to my parents, Donna and Hans, for sacrificing so much of their own time in order to give me the time to write, study and teach. Thanks also to the staff of the Newport Public Library, especially to Luke and Pat, who went above and beyond to help me procure the picture of the WACs used in the "WACs, Workers and Wives" section. For the use of that same photo, thanks also to the *Newport Daily News* and especially to Audrey Hopf for granting the requisite permission. Special thanks also to Mike Slein at the Museum of Newport Irish History for sharing the fascinating laborer's contract that appears in the section entitled "'New' Fort Adams."

Thanks to Doc, for taking the author photo on the spur of the moment and with an unfamiliar camera.

Thanks to my co-author, John, whose idea it was to collaborate on this book; without his years of research on Fort Adams, neither this nor my first book, *True Tales of Life and Death at Fort Adams*, would have been possible.

Finally, thanks are due to the families who donated pictures and memorabilia to the Fort Adams Trust, as well as to those former Fort Adams residents and employees who participated in the 2003

Acknowledgements

Fort Adams Oral History Project. The authors feel strongly that the use of your photos and memories in this book serve the purpose under which many of them were donated: to further the goals of the Fort Adams Trust by educating a wide public about this fascinating and very special place.

PART I

BLOOD AND TREASURE, 1639–1824

THE REVOLUTION

Had it not been for a single winter morning on December 8, 1776, Newport, Rhode Island, would now rival New York as one of the largest, wealthiest and most populous cities on the East Coast of the United States. In its early days, it was well on its way to gaining such a status. The secret to Newport's success was its harbor, the largest and deepest natural port between New York, nearly two hundred miles to the south, and Boston, seventy miles to the north. Since the city's humble beginnings in 1639, when William Brenton and a handful of other gentlemen farmers received grants of fertile land at the southern end of Aquidneck Island from England's King Charles I, Newport had burgeoned into a booming seaport. The thriving comings and goings of mercantile ships—and the economic benefits brought by tacitly sanctioned pirates—placed colonial Newport in the same league as New York, Boston, Philadelphia and Charleston.

There was just one problem: Newport's colonials weren't the only ones who appreciated the blessings of their harbor. As early as the late 1600s, a gun battery centrally located near what is now the corner of Thames and Pelham Streets testified that Newporters had foreseen their most precious resource becoming the envy of some future enemy. From this position, the guns could easily command Newport Harbor and engage any approaching vessels. Over the years, Newport's defenses grew along with the city's importance as a seaport.

In 1703, during Queen Anne's War, the battery at Thames and Pelham was joined by a permanent fortification on Goat Island named Fort Anne in honor of the then-reigning English monarch, ensuring that now not only the harbor but also the approach were covered. The strategic placement of this position made it a long-standing fixture in Newport's defenses, and the small fort was progressively expanded and updated in various incarnations. The story of the young nation's struggle to forge its own identity can be read in the successive names of this single fortification; known as Fort George from 1724 to 1775, another name change signaled a separation from monarchy when the fort was dubbed Fort Liberty in 1775. It would be known by that name until the end of the Revolution and the beginning of independence in 1789, when the name changed again, to Fort Washington.

Newport was in the sights of the British Royal Navy at the very outbreak of war in 1776. Loyalist and Continental forces alike were convinced that whoever possessed Newport Harbor would command all of New England—and from there the whole eastern seaboard of the American colonies.[1] The war had barely fired its first volleys when, on April 6, 1776, British vessels—no doubt thirsting for justice against the Newporters who had burned the customs enforcer HMS *Liberty* to the waterline in 1769—made their first attempt to seize the port. But on the little peninsula of land that had once been William Brenton's farm, curling toward the harbor and the entrance to Narragansett Bay, a humble artillery earthwork armed with four cannons[2] was made ready for the assault.

In the first encounter, the guns of the Newport Artillery Company, under the command of Colonel Richmond, drove back the invading HMS *Glasgow* with thirty-five shots fired in the space of thirty minutes.[3] Another rain of cannon fire on April 10 beat the Royal Navy vessels into retreat; they cut their anchor cables and backed off to the shore of Jamestown, the small settlement on Conanicut Island, Newport's neighbor across the East Passage of Narragansett Bay. The guns of Brenton's Point fired on His Majesty's navy a third time, engaging the HMS *Scarborough* and HMS *Cimetar* on April 14 and delivering Newport from the threat of invasion.[4] Temporarily safe, Rhode Island proclaimed its independence from the king of England on

May 4, two months to the day before its sister colonies would take the same history-altering step.

Eight months later, however, on December 8, 1776, the British warships outwitted the sharp eyes of the Newport artillerymen at the Brenton's Point earthworks by sailing up the bay's west passage on the other side of Jamestown, where there was nary a defensive battery in sight, and coming around Conanicut Island's northern tip. The ships landed and disgorged the British Twenty-second Regiment, whose members immediately made themselves comfortable in private citizens' homes throughout the city. They would outstay their welcome for the next three years.

All of Newport's defensive batteries were seized and placed under British command, including the earthworks at Brenton's Point. At last, in July 1778, French sails were spotted on the horizon, moving inexorably toward the entrance to Narragansett Bay at Newport. Charles Hector, Comte d'Estaing, had arrived as the colonies' ally, bringing the French navy to the relief of the occupied city and its harbor. After successfully blockading Aquidneck Island to the south, the French expressed plans to expel the British from Newport by force in an outright invasion. When the British got wind of this, they took the threat seriously enough to scuttle their own vessels in a bid to make the harbor impassable—a desperate move that caused them massive loss of transportation and firepower.

The British were now stranded in the city and surrounded by hostile forces. Technically, Newport was still occupied. The French had the upper hand, and for a time, it seemed that Newport might be liberated at last. Ultimately, though, the French initiative was hampered by status-seeking among their commanders D'Estaing and the Marquis de Lafayette; the rescue effort essentially ended altogether in August. On the ninth of that month, British naval reinforcements under Admiral Howe entered the waters off Newport, and a firefight between the French and British forces ensued. The French came off worse in the engagement, and before they could rally, the damage their vessels had sustained in battle was compounded by a brutal two-day storm. In order to repair their ships—and to avoid further engagement with Howe—the French departed Rhode Island waters and sailed to Boston on August 20, abandoning Newport once again to the mercy of the now increasingly strengthening British presence. Soon after D'Estaing's departure, Continental forces besieged Newport by land in an alternative attempt to free the city but were routed northward right across Aquidneck Island and over the Sakonnet River in the August 29 Battle of Rhode Island.[5]

The grip of the Crown's regiments did not let up until 1779, when the redcoat troops were called away from Newport to reinforce positions in the southern colonies. Their departure, however, failed to lift the pall of despair that their occupation had laid over the city. Three years of one of the harshest occupations of the war left Newport's economy devastated. It would recover feebly and briefly in the early 1800s, only to be crushed again by the British blockade of the War of 1812. After that, Newport would never regain its prominence as a major economic center.

Although Newport ceased to possess the kind of economic significance an enemy nation would seek, the harbor remained a tempting target for future enemies wishing to establish a base for a massive fleet of warships.[6] If Newport were ever taken again, the East Coast cities of the fledgling nation—New York, Boston, even the capital at Washington—would be in danger. The new nation had been established, and now it needed defending. Accordingly, in 1794, America's ally, France, then possessing the greatest army and hence the greatest expertise in military engineering in the world, sent one of its best engineers, Major Stephen Rochefontaine, to plan a series of fortifications along the northeast coastline. After visiting Newport, Rochefontaine determined that Newport Harbor and Narragansett Bay should be defended by a group of forts. One of his first steps was to arm Fort Washington with twenty cannons and to order four guns on traveling carriages to be placed in various locations around Newport, ready for quick transport in the event that an emergency action became necessary.

In July 1794, Fort Washington on Goat Island became the first Newport site officially garrisoned by a company of U.S. Army artillerists and engineers, marking the beginning of the federal military presence in Newport that continues to this day. This was complemented by Fort Greene in the waterfront district known as the Point,[7] the rotund Fort Louis on a rocky outcropping called the Dumplings off Jamestown,[8] Fort Hamilton on Rose Island[9] and the site of the earthworks at Brenton's Point. These and others built during the same era became known as the First System fortifications.[10]

Between May 2 and October 30, 1799, the United States Army purchased three parcels of land on Brenton's Point from one Susanna

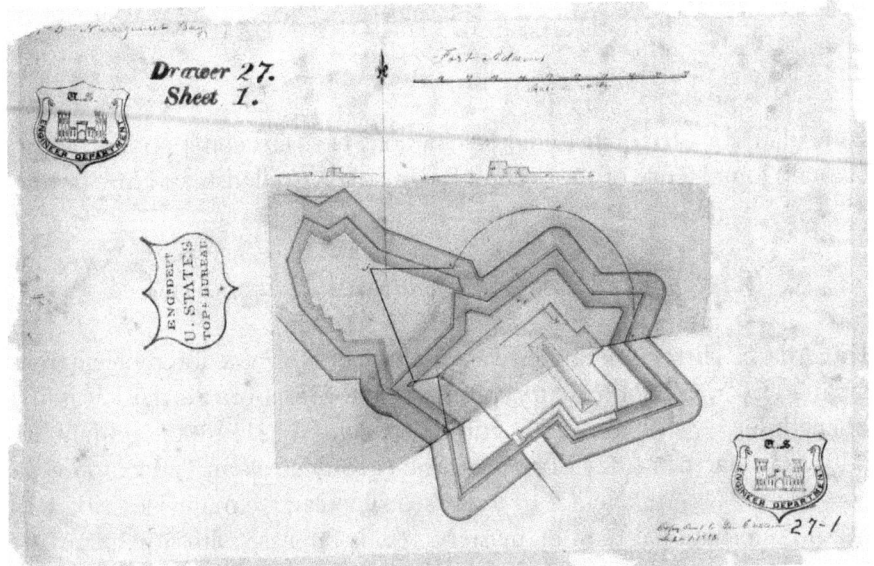

The original Fort Adams of 1799. *National Archives/Bolling W. Smith Collection.*

Mumford.[11] By the time the three successive transactions had been completed, the army would possess more than twenty total acres on the site. After one year of construction, a small brick fort mounting seventeen 32-pounder cannons was built on the very spot where the Newport Artillery Company had fought back the ships of the Royal Navy twenty-three years before. Louis Tousard, another Frenchman who had served as a volunteer with the Continental army, was responsible for its design.[12] Commissioned on July 4, America's birthday, the new fort was christened in honor of the president then in office, John Adams. Major Tousard himself presided over the commissioning ceremony, and the artillery company, which had more than twenty years before fired desperate shots in anger for the defense of the harbor, now fired blank salute volleys. Above the fort's main gate, a sign announced that this was "Fort Adams: The Rock on Which the Storm Will Beat."[13]

The Rock: Old Fort Adams

Fort Adams boasted quite a colorful character as its first commanding officer: Captain John Henry, of the Second Regiment of Artillerists and Engineers.[14]

Captain John Henry: International Man of Mystery

Fort Adams's first commander was the stuff of which action movie heroes are made. Captain John Henry commanded the fort from the day it was first opened, July 4, 1799, until sometime between July 21, 1800, and January 1801. He has been described by various sources as an "adventurer," a "spy" and a "secret agent." In today's vernacular, we might describe him as an "international man of mystery." As is the case with any enigmatic persona, Henry's origins are shrouded in obscurity, without very much authoritative documentation. It is believed that the blond, five-foot-nine anti-hero was born in Ireland in about 1776 and arrived in the States in the late 1790s. If this information is true, it immediately raises a question: why would a twenty-two-year-old of foreign birth be given a commission as a captain in the United States Army almost immediately upon his arrival? It's not likely to have come from the influence of the British minister to the young United States (as some sources claim), since independence had been gained only fifteen years earlier.

Henry's army service was brief, lasting only from June 1, 1798, until December 31, 1801. This coincided with the quasi-war with France during which the U.S. Army and U.S. Navy expanded rapidly—they just as rapidly contracted at the end of hostilities. Henry seems to have been stationed at four different forts during this time: the fort on Bedloe's Island in New York Harbor (now the location of the Statue of Liberty) from June 1798 to sometime early in 1799; Fort Wolcott in Newport from early 1799 to July 4 of that same year; Fort Adams from its commissioning on July 4, 1799, to late 1800; and Fort Sumner in Portland, Maine, from January to December 1801.

On May 23, 1799, Henry married Elizabeth Sophia Duché, the daughter of a prominent Episcopalian priest in Philadelphia. She bore him two daughters before her untimely death in 1808. Upon leaving the army, Henry moved to Vermont to study law. Apparently, he disapproved of the representative republic form of government in the United States and began to make contact with New England Federalists opposed to the Republican Madison administration. These dissenters harbored a desire to break New England away from the United States and, possibly, even restore part of the fledgling nation to British rule.

In about 1809, Henry entered into correspondence with Sir James Craig, the British governor-general of Canada. In this exchange of letters, Henry indicated that many New Englanders would be happy to become British subjects once more. Whether Henry's assessment was accurate, and if so to what degree, it is difficult to say; nevertheless, it was Henry's hope that the Crown would give him lucrative employment in exchange for his providing this kind of potentially vital information. For reasons that are unclear, though, the British government did not find Henry's information of sufficient interest to provide him the position and influence for which he had hoped. As a result, Henry was left with a number of letters from the governor-general that, at the very least, indicated some interest in determining the sentiments of New Englanders toward the U.S. government, as well as the potential for British meddling in the internal affairs of the United States.

Here enters another enigmatic individual into the story: Count Edouard de Crillon. De Crillon's origins are as mysterious as Henry's, and only one thing is certain about him: despite his name, he was not a French count. A whole chapter could be written about De Crillon himself; it was the opinion of noted American historian Henry Adams in 1895 that De Crillon was a con man who was possibly, if not probably, in the employ of Emperor Napoleon Bonaparte.[15]

Napoleon's potential involvement in the matter makes sense when the situation is viewed in a broader international context. In early 1812, Napoleon was preparing for the invasion of Russia, which began on June 24, 1812—coincidentally (or perhaps not so coincidentally) only six days after President Madison signed the declaration of war against the United Kingdom. As Napoleon was going to have the bulk of his army far from France, it was in his interest to have one of his enemies, the United Kingdom, tied down in a war far from France. Therefore, a war between the United States and United Kingdom would serve Napoleon's interests quite well.

Somehow, De Crillon made the acquaintance of John Henry and sensed the latter's anger and frustration at not being rewarded for his efforts on behalf of the British Crown. De Crillon convinced Henry to sell his letters to President James Madison, who was at that moment seeking to build public support for his declaration of war against England.

Henry took De Crillon's advice. He sold his correspondence to Madison on February 7, 1812, for the princely sum of $50,000—more than $1 million in today's currency. Henry had originally asked for eighteen thousand pounds sterling, equivalent to $90,000 then, but $50,000 was the entire "Secret Service" budget that President Madison was authorized to expend. De Crillon then offered to secure a future payment of an additional $40,000 on the United States' behalf by giving Henry the deed to his estate in France. After the deal was struck and the letters handed over, Henry sailed from New York to France on March 10 aboard the warship USS *Wasp*.

The day before Henry sailed, President Madison sent a message regarding his communications to the House of Representatives:

Congress—House of Representatives
Monday, March 9, 1812

The following message was received from the President of the U. States

To the Senate and House of Representatives.

I lay before Congress copies of certain documents which remain in the department of state. They prove that at a recent period, whilst the U. States, notwithstanding the wrong sustained by them, ceased not to observe the laws of peace and neutrality towards G. Britain; and in the midst of amicable professions and negotiations on the part of the British government, through her public minister here, a secret agent of that government was employed in certain states, more especially at the seat of government (Boston) in Massachusetts, in fermenting [sic] disaffection to the constituted authorities of the nation, and in intrigues with the disaffected, for the purpose of bringing about resistance to the laws; and eventually in concert with a British force, of destroying the Union and forming the Eastern part thereof into a political connection with G. Britain.

In addition to the effect which the discovery of such a procedure ought to have on the public councils, it will not fail to render more dear to the hearts of all good citizens that happy union of these states, which under Divine Providence, is the guarantee of their liberties, their safety, their tranquility and their prosperity.

James Madison[16]

While Madison would get his desired declaration of war against the United Kingdom in June, the antiwar Federalist party response is summed up in the following verse: "The Henry Papers, bought and sold, and paid for with the nation's gold."[17]

There is little information about Henry's life after leaving the United States. Apparently, De Crillon's estate in France was a fabrication—perhaps a front—and Henry was last known to have been employed by King George IV of England to spy on his wayward wife, Caroline of Brunswick, in the hopes of gaining sufficient evidence to divorce her on grounds of adultery. Henry is believed to have died in Paris in 1853.

Fort Adams's first commanding officer was certainly a complex man. Although there are more questions about his life than available answers, he may be summed up in the words of nineteenth-century historian Henry Adams: "He was a political blackmailer, an adventurer; and, like a good many of his political superiors, more or less a liar."[18] Ironically, this same Henry Adams, who provided such biographical information as we have concerning De Crillon and John Henry, was the great-grandson of President John Adams, for whom Fort Adams was named on July 4, 1799—the day Captain John Henry became its first commanding officer.

Changes on the Horizon

In 1802, reductions in the army consolidated into a single unit the two artillery companies assigned to Newport. These were stationed not at Fort Adams but rather at the fortification on Goat Island, at this point known as Fort Wolcott. As a result, Fort Adams's garrison moved out, and the fort would be unmanned for the next decade. In 1812, as the threat of invasion by British warships once more loomed on the horizon beyond Narragansett Bay, Fort Adams would be called into service again. By July 1814, history seemed about to repeat itself as British vessels began operating off the coast of New England. This time, though, Newport would be ready.

Wood's State Corps, under the command of the eponymous Major John Wood, and comprising three companies of Rhode Island militiamen—about three hundred in all—was garrisoned at Fort Adams in anticipation of an invasion. But although the British blockaded the coastline, an actual invasion never came—perhaps because the British were aware that Newport had improved its defenses and that occupation would be a greater challenge than it had been during the previous conflict. Nevertheless, Wood's State Corps remained at the fort, serving dutifully to the end of the war and its release from service in 1815.

Two years after this war's end, Fort Adams hosted the newly inaugurated president James Monroe, who made a stop at the fort while touring the northern states. Reporting the event, the *Newport Mercury* claimed that "[i]n the course of the day, the president visited and inspected the garrisons of Forts Wolcott and Adams, with the order and neatness of which, he expressed himself highly gratified."[19]

Although Newport was spared the ravages of the enemy this time, the British did land farther south at Washington, and royal troops razed the young capital to the ground. After the United States declared victory, the federal government was spurred to action. Congress established a Fortifications Board in 1816 to develop a series of defenses along the entire eastern seaboard. This was the beginning of the Coast Artillery Corps of the United States Army.

Still remembering the part Newport Harbor had played in the Revolution—and the part it came too close to playing in the War of 1812—the Fortifications Board selected the city as one of the locations whose defenses would receive a facelift. The old Fort Adams was declared inadequate to properly defend the area in case of attack, and by the early 1820s, it was falling into disrepair. Rather than shore it up, the board decided to tear it down and start from scratch to construct the largest and most complex fortification in North America at that time—a defensive work so intimidating that none would dare attack it. On February 7, 1821, the Engineer Board of the federal government expressed the necessity of its plan to construct state-of-the-art, ultra-strong defenses of Rhode Island's major waterway:

> *The projected defenses of Narragansett Bay will deprive an enemy of the possibility of occupying that excellent road-stead, and secure it to the United States. The procession* [sic] *of this Bay will be to us of inestimable advantage. If Narragansett Bay was left in its existing state, as to defense, an enemy would seize it without difficulty, and, by aid of his naval supremacy, form an establishment in Rhode Island for the war. He might then defy all the forces of the eastern states; drive the United States to vast expense of blood and treasure; and, while his troops would thus put in alarm and motion all the population of the east, feigned*

expeditions against New York, by Long Island Sound, would equally alarm that state and the neighboring ones; and, if he merely contented himself with menacing the coast, it is difficult to calculate the expenses into which he would drive the government.[20]

By safeguarding Newport Harbor to prevent any future enemy from establishing a base, the new Fort Adams would indirectly defend the entire East Coast for the next 125 years, through five future wars.[21] Boston, New York, Charleston and Washington, D.C., itself would owe their security to this massive artillery fortress standing guard at the southern tip of Rhode Island, even though it would never see a single shot from a single enemy gun.

"NEW" FORT ADAMS

By 1824, asking assistance from America's longtime ally, France, was becoming something of a standby, if not an outright habit. It was a fortunate friendship. In the 1820s, although England boasted the greatest navy in the world, the greatest army belonged to France. It made sense that the young United States would model its own army on that of the nation that had provided aid toward the victories of the Revolution. When the Fortifications Board was established in 1816, France's greatest military engineer was Baron Simon Bernard, alumnus of Paris's École Polytechnique, student of French masters of military design Vauban and Montalembert and, at one time, Napoleon Bonaparte's lieutenant general of engineers.

Bernard's expertise was not just academic and theoretical, though. In 1813, under Napoleon, he had directed the defense of Torgau, Saxony, with eight thousand men at his command, superintending the defense of that city during a terrible three-month siege. American president James Monroe felt that there was no better candidate than this battle-baptized nobleman for the position of chief designer, and he offered the job to Bernard with the enticement of receiving the pay and honorary rank of brigadier general in return for his services as engineer for the U.S. Army. Bernard accepted and would continue to serve in this capacity until 1831.[22]

Above: Brigadier General Baron Simon Bernard, who served as a military engineer under Napoleon and designed Fort Adams and Fort Monroe. *Fort Adams Trust.*

Opposite: Simon Bernard's original design for Fort Adams, as drafted by Guillaume Tell Poussin. Colonel Totten later modified this design. *National Archives/Bolling W. Smith Collection.*

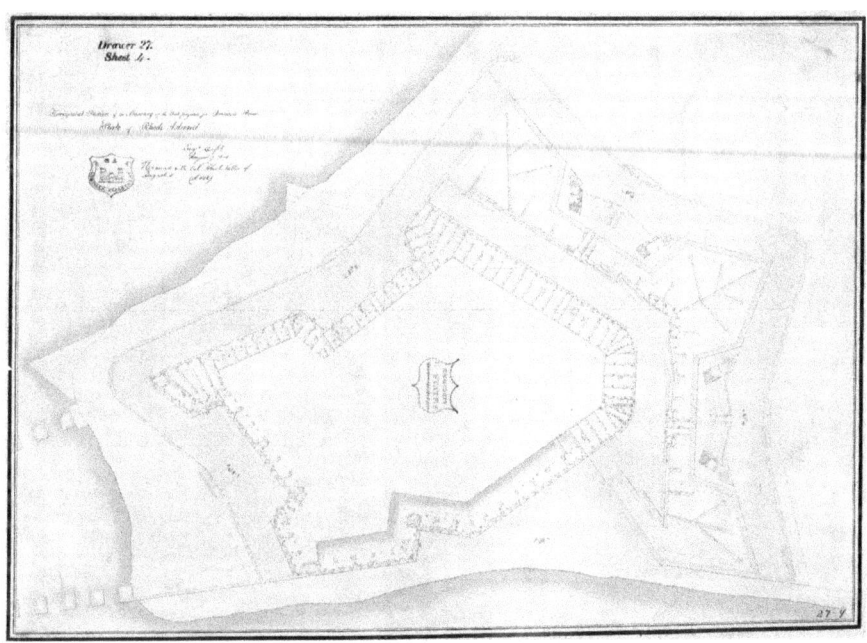

Bernard's legacy lasts to this day in the East Coast forts he designed, known as the Third System fortifications. These descendants of the castles and fortified towns of the Middle Ages brought the centuries-tested credentials of European defense design to American shores. But Bernard was not alone in his efforts. America's own military engineering genius, an 1805 graduate of the military academy at West Point named Joseph G. Totten, assisted Bernard in the design and execution of the new defenses. After the departure of the first supervisor of construction at the new Fort Adams (First Lieutenant Andrew Talcott of the Army Corps of Engineers), Totten took over as superintendent in 1825 and would remain at the fort for the next thirteen years, leaving that post only to take up a new one as chief engineer of the U.S. Army in 1838.[23] Totten was soon promoted from major to lieutenant colonel, and Fort Adams would become one of his least famous masterpieces—not for any defect in its design but rather for its absence from history textbooks, having never participated in any historic battle.[24]

Totten was assisted in his task by several fellow West Point alumni, now lieutenants in the Army Corps of Engineers and eager to make their marks. John G. Barnard would go on to command the defenses of Washington, D.C., during the Civil War, and George W. Cullum would cap his career as superintendent of his alma mater, West Point. But the most ironic of Totten's

Fort Adams

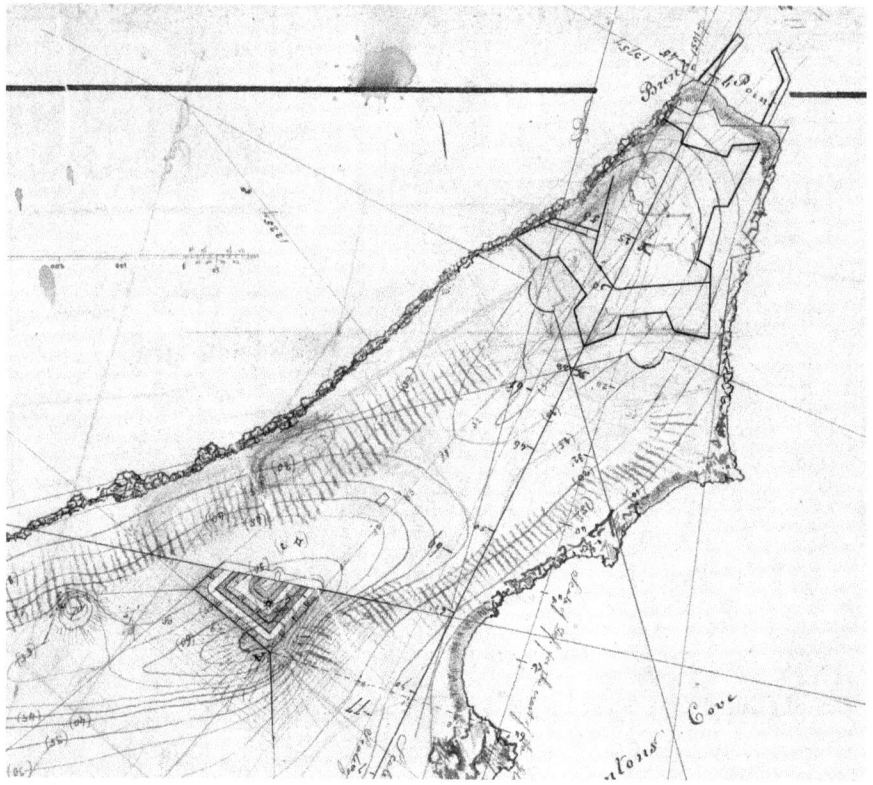

This intriguing diagram shows the outline of the 1799 Fort Adams within the parade field of the 1824 fort. *National Archives/Bolling W. Smith Collection.*

associations by far was a young man named Pierre G.T. Beauregard, whose appointment to Fort Adams marked his very first posting in the army. Long after he had left Fort Adams behind, Beauregard would remain loyal to the Virginian secession and, as a general in the Confederate army, go on to command the attack on Fort Sumter, igniting the spark that began the whole seemingly endless horror of the Civil War. He would not be the only man who represented Fort Adams's presence in that conflict. But in 1825, when Sumter was still thirty-five years in the future, there was no reason for relations between the West Point comrades to be anything but friendly.

Even after Totten's departure from Fort Adams, his interest in that project never faded. On August 20, 1840, Totten returned to inspect the fort and was apparently pleased that its progress was continuing along lines he had established.

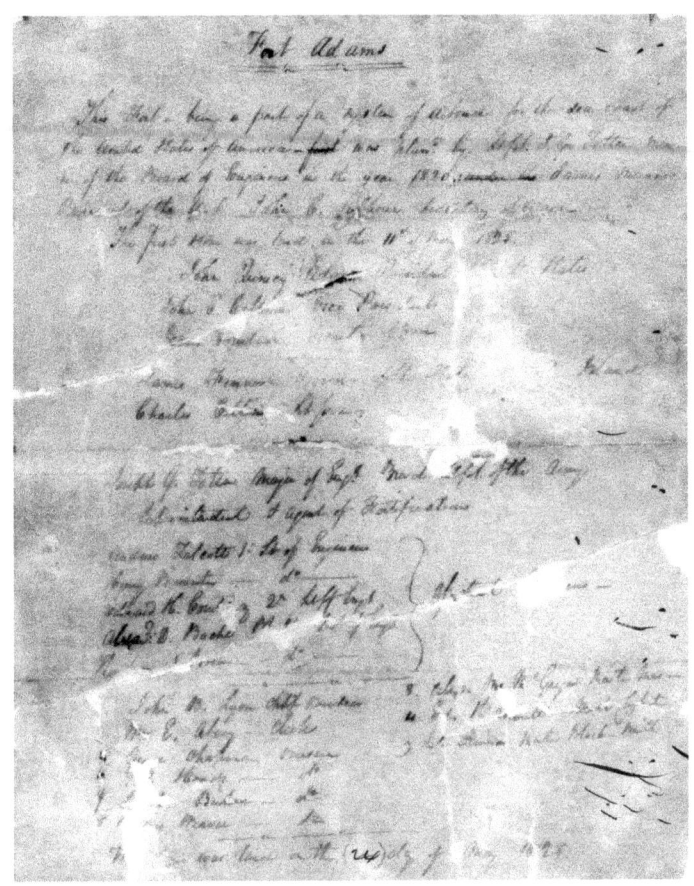

Fort Adams's "birth certificate." *National Archives/ Bolling W. Smith Collection.*

Totten's memory remained active at Fort Adams years after his death. In 1905, while undertaking extensive improvements and alterations to bring Fort Adams up to date, workmen somehow shattered the original cornerstone of the fort. Inside, they discovered an old document, placed in the cornerstone in 1825, that read, in part, as follows:

This fort, being a part of the system of defence [sic] for the seacoast of the United States of America, was planned by Lieut. Col. J.G. Totten, member of the Board of Engineers in the year 1820; James Monroe, President of the United States; John C. Calhoun, Vice President; James Barber, Secretary of War. The first stone was laid on the 11th of May, 1825.[25]

This invaluable record might be called Fort Adams's "birth certificate."

Bernard and Totten's design was brought to life by Scotsman Alexander MacGregor, the master mason who oversaw the construction of the fort's stonework. After completing his task at Fort Adams, MacGregor spent the rest of his life in Newport and passed away in the city in 1870. The versatility of MacGregor's talent is on display in his other projects of note in Newport, including the Perry Mill, the Newport Artillery armory and the Swanhurst mansion on Bellevue Avenue—all very different structures, reflecting that MacGregor's abilities ranged from fortifications to industrial buildings to private residences.[26]

Fort Adams, Religious Freedom and the American Dream

If men like Bernard, Totten and MacGregor could be called the collective brain behind Fort Adams, there had to also be muscle that made their vision reality. The manpower that drove Fort Adams to completion was fueled by the sweat of immigrant labor, chiefly from economically depressed Ireland. Irishmen had begun seeking a better life in the new United States before Fort Adams, of course; in Rhode Island, the coal mines in Portsmouth, at the farther end of Aquidneck Island from Newport, had attracted a great number of Irish miners, and many of them later found work on the crew at Fort Adams.[27] But soon they were joined by their countrymen across the Atlantic who answered U.S. Army advertisements for free passage to America and gainful employment building the largest structure in North America up to that time.

The labor force varied in number from time to time, but always the number of workers who could be seen toiling at the block-and-tackle works was in the hundreds. At the peak of construction in 1836, five hundred laborers constituted the whole crew. They were paid approximately one dollar per day for work that was backbreaking and sometimes fatal—at least two workers were killed while constructing the fort's underground tunnels: John Butler of Boston in August 1825 and John Tracy in March 1827.[28] In September 1836, a scaffold collapsed and nearly killed the man working on it; the following month, laborer Michael Quin may as well have been killed when he lost his right arm in a rock-blasting accident—for a laborer in the nineteenth century, losing an arm was a fate equal to death.[29]

FORT-ADAMS,
Newport Harbour, June 2d, 1831.
THE following Regulations, as to hours of labour, will be hereafter observed at this Work :—

It is requested that all Mechanics or Labourers who may feel unwilling to comply therewith, will give notice to that effect without delay, so that their places may be supplied.

The Bell will ring for Morning Roll-call at 6 o'clock A. M. from the 20th of March to the 20th of September, inclusive; and at Sunrise from the 21st September to the 19th March inclusive.

The Bell for leaving off Morning work will ring at 12 o'clock, (Noon) throughout the Year.

The Bell for Afternoon Roll-call will ring at 1 o'clock P. M. throughout the Year.

The Bell for leaving off Afternoon work will ring at sundown throughout the Year.

The time of labour will be divided into quarters of days as follows:—Between the 20th of March and 20th of September, the first Quarter from 6 to 9 A. M.—the second Quarter from 9 to 12 o'clock—the third Quarter from 1 to 4 P. M.—and the fourth Quarter from 4 P. M. to Sunset.——Between the 21st Sept. and 19th March, the first Quarter from Sunrise to half past 9 A. M.—the second Quarter from half past 9 to 12 o'clock—the third Quarter from 1 to 3 P. M.—and the fourth Quarter from 3 P. M. to Sunset.

Whenever the weather is so unfavorable that the Work cannot proceed with advantage, all Mechanics and Labourers will be called off by the ringing of the Bell. Should this happen before half past 7 o'clock of the 1st quarter—half past 10 o'clock of the 2d quarter—half past 2 o'clock of the 3d quarter—and half past 4 o'clock of the 4th quarter, no time will be allowed on the Rolls for that Quarter—but should the Workmen not be called off till after the times just specified, the full quarter will be allowed.

No Person absent at Roll-call will, in any case, be allowed credit for the Quarter then commencing; nor will any Person, so absent, be credited for the next quarter, unless he shall report himself in person, to the first Overseer, or the Master Mechanic, or the sub-Overseer, under whom he may be at work, in time to commence with the next Quarter.

No Person can be credited for either of the Quarters if he break off work before the expiration thereof—and no person can be credited for the 1st or 3d quarter, if he break off work at the expiration thereof without reporting the same at the time, to the sub-Overseer under whose superintendence he may be labouring, or to the 1st Overseer whose duty it will be before crediting the person for such Quarter, to ascertain that the Quarter had fully expired, before he quitted work.

It must be distinctly understood that no excuse can be received for not being present before the calling of the Roll is completed.

All Master-Workmen, and Sub-Overseers, must be present at Roll-call.

Payment, in full, will be made to any person employed at this Work, whenever he may desire it—and at the beginning of every Month all arrears of the preceeding Month will be settled.

Previous to making up the Rolls at the end of each Month, the 1st Overseer will prepare a statement of the time credited to each person, and will read it to the Workmen at one of the Roll-calls, to satisfy them that the time is correctly stated, and to enable them to have mistakes rectified, should any have been committed.

The time at this Fort will be regulated by the State-House Clock in Newport; and the 1st Overseer and Master-Mason will both be careful to keep their Watches agreeing with that Clock.

Whenever the rising or setting of the Sun is obscured, the times of sunrise and sunset will be taken from the Almanack.

As heretofore, the time to be credited to each Man will be kept by the Master-Mechanics and Sub-Overseers, and be by them reported, daily, to the 1st Overseer.

A Copy of these Regulations will be given to every Man employed upon this Work;—his Name, the Date, and the price at which he is hired, being first written in the blanks below, by the 1st Overseer, or the Master-Mason, as the case may be.

Fort Adams, June 20 1831. John Quigley is hired this day as a _____ at One 00/100 Dollar per day.

Copy of a contract hiring Irishman John Quigley to work on Fort Adams. Donated to the Museum of Newport Irish History by Quigley's descendant David Cummings. *Museum of Newport Irish History.*

While many of the Irish who had worked on the fort departed to find more work when their time on the crew was done, some remained, giving Fort Adams a role in Newport's long and proud Irish heritage, which included a testament to the city's tradition of religious diversity. Roman Catholicism had come to Newport's shores during the Revolution with the arrival of Hessian and later French troops, but the religion did not maintain a strong presence thereafter. Despite Newport's long history of free worship for a variety of faiths, Catholics began a prominent and permanent presence in the city for the first time only with the men who built Fort Adams.

The first Roman Catholic parish in the state of Rhode Island was begun by the Boston archdiocese in 1828 specifically to serve the hundreds of Irish families whose men were laboring on the fort. After a small beginning, using an adapted building to gather for Mass once a month, the congregation built a larger church dedicated to St. Joseph in 1833. When the Catholic population outgrew even that structure, the neo-Gothic brownstone church officially called the Holy Name of Mary, Our Lady of the Isle ("St. Mary's" for short), was constructed on the corner of Spring Street and Memorial Boulevard between 1848 and 1852. The same men who built Fort Adams worked also to build this house of worship, partially using leftover construction materials from the fort. The presence of this church announced not only the new establishment of an ancient faith but also the fact that the Irish now claimed Newport as their home. In 1953, the church would gain fame as the venue for the wedding of future president John F. Kennedy and his wife, Jacqueline—a fitting venue for the wedding of the first president of both Irish ancestry and Catholic faith. To this day, a small gold plate marks pew number ten as the favored seat of the ill-fated president when he attended Mass during his summer visits to his in-laws' Newport estate, Hammersmith Farm.[30]

Alexander MacGregor ensured that the fort's walls provided impregnability as well as an intimidating appearance, constructed of a masterful combination of gray shale (much of this native stone acquired on-site in the process of excavating and blasting to create the fort's foundations) and Maine granite shipped to Newport by schooner.[31] A special dock was built right at the tip of Brenton's Point, at the fort's north side, to bring in the rough granite blocks and haul them up the quays to be shaped on-site according to whatever size and shape stone block might be called for. In their day, those walls were built to withstand the mightiest

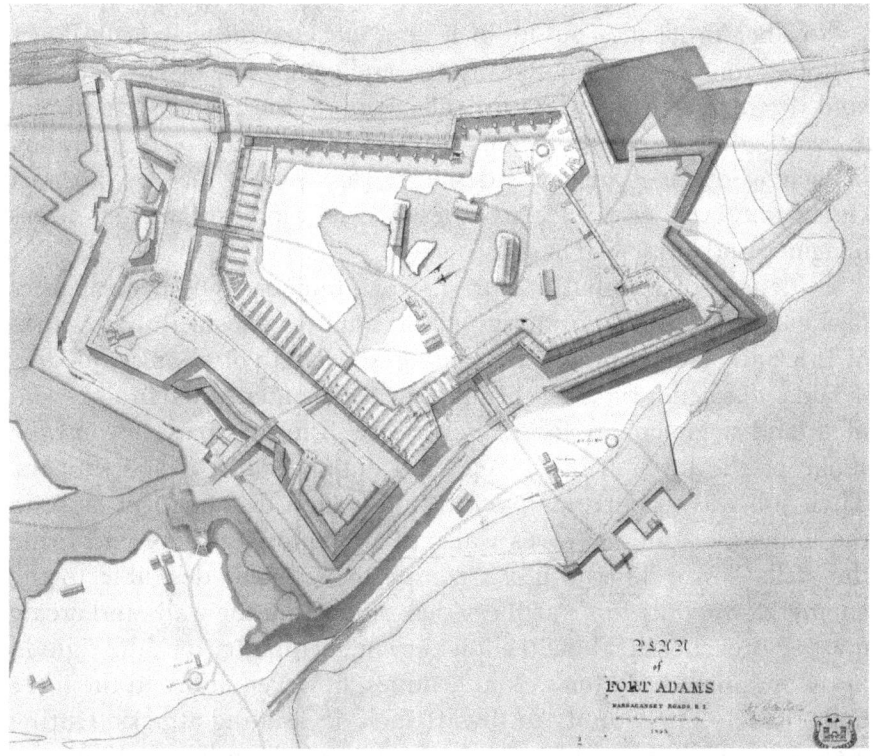

Fort Adams plan of work, 1833. *National Archives/Bolling W. Smith Collection.*

barrage of the enemy. Should any hostile warship approach, its cannon fire would deflect harmlessly off Fort Adams's great stone perimeter of 1,700 yards. Only the perimeter of Fortress Monroe in Virginia is larger, allowing Fort Adams only one rival in the whole country.

Fort Adams was intended to be the most formidable defensive position on the entire eastern seaboard of the young United States, capable of supporting a garrison of 2,400 troops and an artillery complement of 468 cannons. One of the first features to be completed was the outer defenses extending almost a mile to the south of the fort proper, the only direction from which the fort could be approached over land. Paired with the unparalleled firepower of the west curtain's 117 cannons guarding the entrance to Newport Harbor at Narragansett Bay's East Passage, deterring attack from the sea, the land defenses made Fort Adams an impregnable obstacle to any enemy occupation of the harbor and the city of Newport.[32]

No other fortification outside of Europe (not even the technically larger Fortress Monroe) can rival the vastness and complexity of Fort Adams's land defenses. This area in particular demonstrates that Bernard and (especially) Totten took quite literally every possibility into consideration in their work. As if the fort's design process were a massive, abstract chess game, every tactic of a hypothetical enemy force by land or sea was imagined and forestalled in construction.

Evidence of Totten's mastery of military engineering lies particularly in the elaborate system of countermines within networks of brick and stone tunnels, amounting to a length of about 2,500 feet if laid end to end, running through the fort's outer walls. In the event of a land siege, enemy forces would establish their base beyond the range of the fort's artillery and send out specialists called sappers. Their job was to burrow underground from a distance, get close to the foundations of the fort's walls, plant explosives there and bring the walls down. This would accomplish two goals desirable to the enemy: destroy the fort's artillery defenses within the walls and create massive breaches that would allow the enemy infantry to waltz right in fairly unopposed. Totten's countermines, however, afforded the fort's defenders an opportunity to thwart such devastating attacks. During a siege, defenders would man the brick tunnels to listen closely for any sound that might signal the sappers' approach. Should the men hear those sounds, the defenders would plant their own explosives at the countermines and retreat, collapsing the wall at strategic points that would stop the sappers' advance and leave the wall above intact, along with the artillery within.

In addition, shorter "safe passage" tunnels ran underground across the fort's interior and exterior ditches. If a skirmish were taking place in the ditches, and the fort's defenders needed to reinforce the rifle galleries in the outer walls or to retreat from those galleries back into the fort proper, these tunnels allowed them to do so without being exposed to harm by gunfire and shrapnel. It was the creation of these underground "safe transport" tunnels that proved most problematic for the laborers' safety. When construction began on the new fort in 1824, the engineering technology did not exist, as it does now, to simply build the tunnels through the earth. The soil had to first be completely excavated, then the tunnels were constructed and finally the earth was placed back over the finished tunnels. It is very likely that the unfortunate laborers Butler and Tracy were killed when engaged in this work.[33]

Fort Adams received a visit from the son of its namesake on October 13, 1826, when President John Quincy Adams visited Newport and made a point of stopping at the fort that bore his father's name. Colonel Totten himself gave the president a tour of the fort's progress in construction.[34]

It was not until 1841, though, when the fort had been under construction for nearly twenty years and Totten had been gone for three years, that the "new" Fort Adams was finally garrisoned, by Companies F and I of the Second Artillery Regiment under commanding officer Major Matthew M. Payne. Their first large "engagement" would occur on July 26, 1842, in the form of a mock battle, the first of many that would occur at the fort throughout its history and one enjoyed by Newport's civilian population, which was always invited to witness such spectacles not only as a great entertainment but likely also to impress the populace with the prowess of the military forces that stood ready for the city's defense. (It also wouldn't hurt, no doubt, to remind civilians, some of whom might have been able to remember the Revolution sixty years after its end, that their tax money was being well spent.)

PART II
THE WARS OF THE NINETEENTH CENTURY

THE MEXICAN-AMERICAN WAR, 1845–1848

Fort Adams continued unassailed during the first major war after the Revolution, the Mexican-American War. But that didn't mean that the fort sat idly by. As it would continue to do for the next century, Fort Adams served as a base of deployment, training soldiers and sending them to the front. The closest the fort came to seeing battle was in May 1845, when commanding officer Lieutenant Colonel Benjamin K. Pierce received orders to mount all cannons immediately. The anticipated attack never came, however, and Fort Adams maintained its uninterrupted peace.

In April 1847, six years after being garrisoned but while the fort was still under construction, Fort Adams was designated as a gathering spot for all troops originating in the eastern states; in reality, the only troops to use the fort in this capacity were the men of the Ninth Infantry Regiment, under the command of Colonel Truman B. Ransom of Vermont.

The first batch of soldiers from the Ninth, a company that had been raised in Rhode Island under the command of one Captain Joseph S. Pitman, arrived in Newport on March 11, 1847.[35] The soldiers left for Mexico and the battlefront very shortly thereafter, on March 26, despite Colonel Ransom's attempt to delay their deployment on the grounds that he had not given assent to the order to move them. The next groups of infantry from the Ninth arrived in successive waves between April 26 and May 12. On May 19, Brigadier General Franklin Pierce stopped briefly at Fort Adams on his way to Mexico. While at the fort, the bulk of the Ninth Infantry was still there, awaiting transport to serve in Mexico. Pierce departed Fort Adams on the twenty-eighth, along with the last detachment of the Ninth, and went on to serve with distinction in Mexico. In 1852, Pierce was elected president of the United States but served only one term in that office, from 1853 to 1857.

When the whole regiment was gathered, the men shipped out for Mexico in much the same fashion they had come to Fort Adams: in separate groupings, between May 21 and 28. The Fort Adams–trained troops later saw action at the Battle of Chapultepec, where on September 13 their commander, Colonel Ransom, fell to the enemy while leading his troops. A captain of the Ninth, John S. Slocum, survived the battle and the rest of the war and would go on to become a colonel himself, at the head of the Second Rhode Island Regiment during the early Civil War's First Battle of Bull Run. Fate would lead him to eventually imitate his own commander, Colonel Ransom, in more ways than simply holding the same rank.

It was around this time, in the late 1840s, that Lieutenant Ambrose Burnside was stationed at Fort Adams. Nearly twenty years later, he would gain fame (or infamy, rather) for his questionable performances at the Civil War battles of Fredericksburg and, most especially, Antietam, where a bridge still stands that bears his name—not in honor, but as a byword.

Fort Adams's "Mini-Fort": The Southern Redoubt

During the mid-1800s, the greatest achievement in the fort's construction was the completion of the southern redoubt, a small, fortified defensive position about a quarter of a mile to the south of the fort proper. Its construction was supervised by First Lieutenant Isaac Ingalls Stevens, who would later rise to the rank of brigadier general during the Civil War.[36] The redoubt at Fort Adams is much more than simply a set of thick stone walls. A fort in its own right, it boasts sophisticated features mirroring those of the main fort: outer and inner dry moats, reverse fire galleries, interconnecting tunnel systems and the only dual-spiral staircase on the North American continent. This formidable post covered the southern approach, the only direction from which the fort could be directly assaulted over land. An enemy army would have to deal with this redoubt before even beginning an attack on the main fortification.

In the event that the redoubt was overrun, a retreat was created called the "covered" or "covert" way—not because it was covered with a roof or overhang of any kind but rather because it provided a path for retreating Fort Adams defenders that was "covered" by artillery fire from cannons mounted en barbette atop the walls of the main fort. No sane commander would order his infantry to take the logical next step of assaulting the fort directly. The only access over land was via the *glacis*, a long, upward-sloping grade of land that from the start placed invaders at a disadvantage on low ground, while the fort's defenders occupied the more strategic high ground. The remains of the *glacis* can still be seen today, but the presence of a rugby field and navy housing obscures the fact that this slope was originally a wide-open space. This meant that enemy infantry attempting to traverse the *glacis* would be completely exposed to artillery fire from atop the fort's outer walls. Any force approaching over land would be handily eliminated before getting within half a mile of the fort proper.

Still, the fort's outer defenses weren't taken for granted in its design. On the very slim chance that enemy troops were able to push through to the exterior wall, they would funnel into the interior ditch and face a line of flank howitzers blasting canister shot through their ranks. Horror stories from the Civil War tell of human beings completely obliterated by canister. As the name implies, canister shot was composed of a metal cylinder crafted to explode in midair and scatter its contents—musket balls, rusty nails, bits of scrap metal—at high velocity, shearing through bodies as if they were paper dolls. Men could be vaporized by canister, flesh and bone reduced to a pink mist. That was the greeting that awaited any land force that got that close to Fort Adams. If this wasn't enough, a reverse-fire gallery in the exterior wall would loose rifle volleys onto the enemy from behind. Had Fort Adams ever been assaulted, it would have been a literal bloodbath.[37]

Opposite, top: Aerial view of the redoubt. Note the multiple layers of defense. *John S. and Margaret D. Dugan Collection.*

Opposite, bottom: Redoubt entrance with bridge. *John S. and Margaret D. Dugan Collection.*

The Wars of the Nineteenth Century

Fort Adams

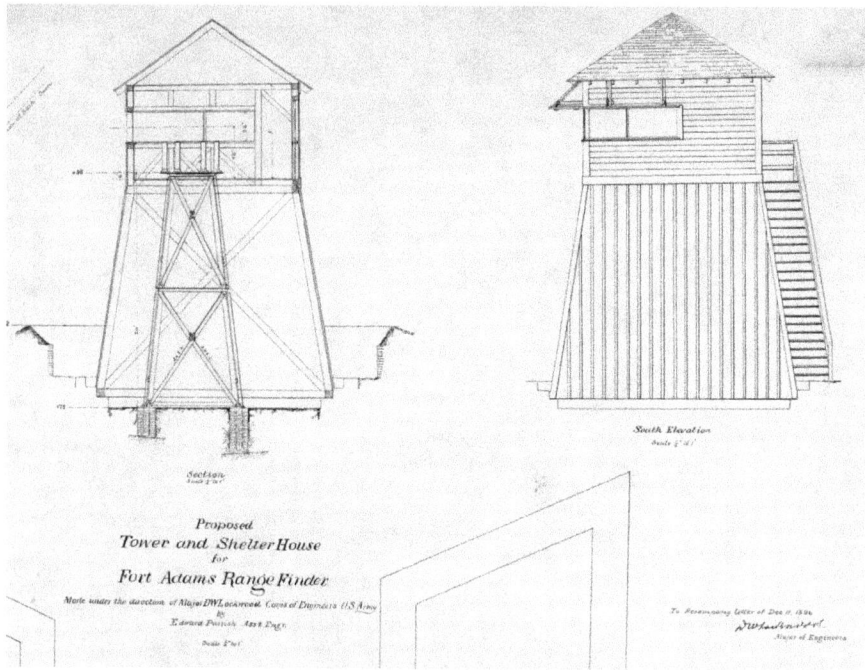

The watchtower atop Fort Adams's southern redoubt. *Library of Congress.*

Northward view from fire control tower on top of the redoubt. Note the row of officers' quarters and radio antennas. *National Archives/Daniel P. Titus Collection.*

But no combat was needed to bring Fort Adams soldiers to their graves. In 1849, the fort was garrisoned by the headquarters and three companies of the Third U.S. Artillery under the command of Colonel William Gates. These companies remained at Fort Adams for the next four years, until new orders summoned them to California in October 1853. Most of the regiment made the trip aboard the SS *San Francisco*. On the way, the ship was struck by a massive wave that swept more than one hundred passengers, including Fort Adams men, to a watery death.

Fort Days

After the departure of the Third Artillery, Fort Adams was placed in caretaking status, without a full-time garrison, until 1857, when Company I of the First Artillery arrived to fill the void. Its commander was Captain John B. Magruder,[38] one of the most flamboyant characters to ever possess a command at Fort Adams. During his tenure at the fort, Magruder brought his native southern hospitality to bear in making Fort Adams a hub of the wider Newport community as a center of social events. He regularly opened the base for "Fort Days," inviting Newport's civilian residents to the fort to enjoy concerts, dances and genteel parties. According to contemporary newspaper accounts, the music generated at these Fort Adams soirées traveled across the harbor and was heard in downtown Newport. One frequent act was a band called the Germanians, which composed the Fort Adams March specially for Colonel Magruder. The colonel's Fort Days turned out to be wildly popular among Newporters and were always well attended. The tradition continued, and in 1886, long after Magruder had departed, the *Newport Mercury* opined that "[t]he most attractive feature of the Fort is undoubtedly the splendid band of the Fourth United States Artillery…During the warm days of summer there can be no more pleasant relief than to sail across to Fort Adams and listen to the charming music of the Fort band."[39]

In keeping with the customs of the culture in which he was raised, however, Magruder's famed hospitality did not extend to all the citizens of the City by the Sea. On one occasion during Magruder's term as commander, a carriage occupied by black Americans attempting to attend one of the Fort Days was summarily turned away. A former resident of the fort, in a reminiscence article in the *Newport Daily News* for July 26, 1901, recalled the incident, and his words deserve to be recounted verbatim:

> *A great commotion was created, on one occasion, by the appearance in the line, in a humble vehicle, of a company of colored ladies and gentlemen, with all the assurance of their lighter colored brethren and sisters. They had not traveled many places before they were discovered by General Magruder, the horse was seized by the head by a couple of soldiers, and the outfit led outside the sally-port and the occupants told to go their way, and not appear again.*[40]

Nor was racism alone among Magruder's character flaws. On September 14, 1863, after Magruder had departed from his post at Fort Adams, the *Newport Daily News* reported that Magruder had been killed by a jealous husband. This early report later turned out to be unfounded, but the opinion offered on the supposed event by the article's anonymous author is very telling: "Those who knew the traitor when he resided in Newport will consider the story far from improbable. Magruder's reputation as a libertine was almost as patent as that which he bore as a drunkard and he certainly deserved a much worse fate than is said to have befallen him."[41]

Magruder is said to have used Fort Dumplings across Narragansett Bay's East Passage as target practice for Fort Adams's guns. Still, the bulk of Fort Dumplings remained until it was finally demolished in November 1898 to make room for a new fortification, Fort Wetherill, which would serve as a sister base to Fort Adams until the end of World War II.

Magruder and Company I departed Fort Adams on October 31, 1859, reverting the fort to caretaker status under the direction of Ordnance Sergeant Mark Wentworth Smith. Colonel Magruder would soon tender his resignation from the U.S. Army in order to take a commission in the army of the Confederacy, in whose service he would rise to the rank of major general and oversee the Department of Texas. Strangely, after the war, Magruder would accept a commission with the same rank in the Mexican army under Emperor Maximilian. He remains the only military man in United States history to serve in the armed forces of three different nations, all while maintaining his American citizenship.

The Civil War

When South Carolina seceded from the Union in late 1860, there was great concern that the animosity between North and South would result in a civil war, and the Federal government began making preparations accordingly. On January 11, 1861, Lieutenant Edson and six ordnance men from Watertown Arsenal arrived to put Fort Adams in order for active use, mounting cannons on carriages and replenishing the fort's stocks of food and ammunition.

Since 1859, Ordnance Sergeant Mark Wentworth Smith had presided over the fort's caretaking detachment. Smith had been born to Joshua Brewster Smyth and Polly Shepherd Smyth on August 20, 1803, in Grafton, Holderness County, New Hampshire. Army records later spelled the name as "Smith," and this rendering stuck. Prior to joining the army at age twenty-three in January 1827, the brunet, blue-eyed, nearly six-foot-tall Smith trained and was employed as a blacksmith. He first enlisted in Boston under Lieutenant E. Sumner, and he would go on to reenlist in November 1831 in Baltimore, likely assigned to Fort McHenry. He made a career of the army, reenlisting many times. In September 1839, July 1844 and May 1849, his reenlistments were all at Fort Trumbull in New London, Connecticut.

Smith earned his rank of ordnance sergeant at Fort Trumbull, serving in that capacity from 1836 to 1849. The rank of ordnance sergeant had only been in existence for a few decades, created in the early nineteenth century for senior noncommissioned officers who were responsible for the maintenance of fortifications and artillery pieces. This position was especially important at forts that were unmanned except for caretaking detachments—exactly the condition of Fort Adams as of 1861. The ordnance sergeant at such a fort had to ensure that the fort's cannons would not fall into disrepair and that the fort would not fall victim to overgrowth or vandalism in the absence of actively training regiments.

Smith reenlisted again on January 25, 1859, under Captain Clitz at New York. The ordnance sergeant was fifty-six years old at the time, and then, as today, soldiers over the age of fifty were a small minority within the army. It was in late September of that year that Smith began his service at Fort Adams. At the outbreak of the Civil War in April 1861, he was still in charge of the small caretaking detachment that had minded

Fort Adams since 1859, and Smith continued to maintain the fort while it was in use as the Naval Academy from May to September 1861.

Smith was still at Fort Adams for his next reenlistment, by Colonel Oliver L. Shepherd, on December 12, 1863. Shepherd was at Fort Adams as commander of the Fifteenth Infantry Regiment of the regular army, which used the fort as a recruiting depot from October 1862 to February 1866. Smith would not remain at Fort Adams for much longer, however. On December 26, 1863, he was transferred back to Fort Trumbull, where he would spend the remainder of his life as caretaker for Trumbull's subpost, Fort Griswold, in Groton, Connecticut.

Smith's final reenlistment was on December 12, 1868, at the age of sixty-five. He died on active duty at Fort Griswold on September 30, 1879, at the age of seventy-six, and is buried beside his wife and two of his sons (one of whom died in the Civil War) at the Ledyard Cemetery in Groton.[42]

Fort Adams began readying for war in January 1861 when commanding officer Cullum began to suspect "that an expedition from abroad [i.e., the Confederacy] might attempt to secure ammunition, &c., from this unprotected fortification."[43] Accordingly, Captain Cullum ordered four soldiers to stand guard until troops could arrive. These early preparations proved justified in April of that year, when Brigadier General Pierre G.T. Beauregard led the assault on Fort Sumter in the first confrontation of the Civil War. Beauregard had been a Fort Adams man himself. His first assignment in the U.S. Army had been a post as assistant to the fort's brilliant designer and superintendent of construction, Joseph Totten.

Inside Fort Sumter, Major Robert Anderson was in command of the defense. Anderson well knew that it was Beauregard on the other side of Charleston Harbor, but rather than experiencing the adrenaline-saturated anticipation of steeling himself to confront a reviled enemy, Anderson's heart was deeply troubled. When he had taught artillery use and strategy at the U.S. Military Academy at West Point, the sixteen-year-old Pierre Beauregard had sat in his classroom. So fond were professor and student of each other, and so well did they work together, that after Beauregard's graduation in 1838—second in his class—Anderson asked the young man to remain at West Point as his personal assistant, and Beauregard agreed.[44] But as with countless other identical relationships, the Civil War placed each man on opposing sides of the deadly conflict escalating between the Union and the newly formed Confederate States of America. At Fort Sumter, Anderson would see his own teachings turned against him.

The friendship between Beauregard and Anderson somehow survived well enough to be reflected in the exchanges between the two men even as Sumter was besieged. On March 8, a full month before the attack, a live-fire practice round traveled from the Confederate Mount Pleasant mortar battery and struck Sumter's wharf. The shot had been accidental and had fallen short of the fort's wall; nevertheless, in true Southern chivalric fashion, Major Stevens rowed to the fort and offered Major Anderson a profound apology. Anderson responded by sending a note to his former student, assistant and friend, strongly suggesting that the line of mortar practice fire be changed: "I hope, therefore, that, to guard against the possibility of such an event (one, I know, that you would never cease to regret), you will issue such orders as are proper in the case…I most earnestly hope that nothing will ever occur to alter, in the least, the high regard and esteem I have for so many years entertained for you."[45] Beauregard sent his reply the following morning: "I regret to learn that the firing from the mortar battery yesterday was so directed as to render the explosion of the shells dangerous to the occupants of Fort Sumter…Let me assure you, major, that nothing shall be wanting on my part to preserve the friendly relations and impressions which have existed between us for so many years."[46]

Beauregard did see to the redirection of the mortars' line of practice fire, but his affection for his former teacher did not prevent the battle that changed the face of America forever. Anderson probably hoped—vainly as it turned out—that Beauregard would not want to precipitate such a conflict. He also hoped that the esteem in which Beauregard held him would cause the brigadier general not to attack a fort commanded by a personal friend. But there was another reason, aside from their friendship, that helps to explain why neither Beauregard nor Anderson was eager for conflict. Both officers knew what was at stake: a direct attack on a Federal fortification would be considered an outright act of war; this, in turn, would lead to the greatest tragedy in American history.

In the end, Beauregard chose loyalty to his state and his nation—that is, the Confederacy—over his personal esteem for his former teacher. When President Lincoln ordered ships to resupply Fort Sumter in early April, Beauregard issued an ultimatum to Anderson to evacuate the fort or it would be bombarded into submission. Anderson's duty was to preserve the honor of his own country—the Union—at all costs, including the cost of personal friendship, and refused. At 4:30 a.m. on April 12, the bombardment began. The first cannon shot fired in the fort's defense was at the hand of a young Union soldier named Peter Rice. After the war, Rice would go on to be stationed at Fort Adams, where he would succumb to a drowning accident in January 1879, leaving his six children fatherless.[47]

Thirty-six hours after the opening bombardment, Anderson surrendered Fort Sumter, but he was granted the privilege of firing a one-hundred-gun salute in honor of the Union flag before it was hauled down. Furthermore, Anderson and his soldiers were not taken as prisoners of war but were instead allowed to return north unmolested. This was in accord with a custom from the age of chivalry in which a besieged fortress could be granted the "honors" of war by allowing the garrison to march out of the fortress unharmed in exchange for surrendering it without bloodshed. Ironically, the only casualties of this tragic drama were two Union soldiers killed and four seriously wounded when there was an accidental explosion of gunpowder during this final salute, which was ended after fifty guns had been fired.

During the war, Beauregard distinguished himself many times on the battlefield and is still considered one of the greatest of the Confederate generals. After the war, he became a successful railroad executive and served as adjutant general of Louisiana. He died in 1893 at the age of seventy-four.

As for Anderson, he was promoted to brigadier general soon after his return north and held several field commands, but with limited success. He never recovered from the stress and traumatic loss of Fort Sumter. While the need to surrender may have been a cause of Anderson's subsequent ill health, there can be no doubt that the added emotional strain of coming under fire from a friend, as well as the knowledge that said friend was attacking his post with the very artillery techniques Anderson had invested years of his life in teaching him, bore the bulk of responsibility for Anderson's decline. He was placed on "waiting orders" for almost two years before he was assigned to Fort Adams as commanding officer in August 1863. The rationale for this placement lies in an 1861 report on "Sickness and Mortality of the Army and Navy of the United States," which found that not only was the New England coast the most beneficial locale for health but also that Fort Adams itself was "the most salubrious military post in the United States."[48] Anderson failed to benefit from these pleasant conditions, however, and only held this post for three weeks before realizing that he was no longer physically (and perhaps emotionally) capable of performing the demanding duties of active service. He soon retired from the army at his own request.

Despite being "retired," however, Anderson was assigned to the staff of the commanding general of the Department of the East in New York from 1863 to 1869. This was probably an assignment with limited responsibilities and was likely given in light of the high esteem in which Anderson was held in the army, especially due to popular acclaim for his defense of Fort Sumter. For that action, he was brevetted to the rank of major general on February 3, 1865.

Anderson fully retired in January 1869 and worked on translating French military manuals into English. He died in the resort city of Nice, France, at the age of sixty-six, on October 26, 1871, and is buried at the cemetery at West Point with many of his fellow officers and students. Beauregard was not among them, having been buried instead in the Army of Tennessee plot of New Orleans's Metairie Cemetery.[49]

Fort Adams Enters the War

When news of the attack on Fort Sumter reached Rhode Island, Governor Sprague ordered the Old Guard of the Newport Artillery Company to stand guard at Fort Adams to deter any would-be saboteurs.[50] The Old Guard stood watch at the fort until May 9, 1861, when the famed frigate USS *Constitution*—also known as "Old Ironsides"—arrived in Narragansett Bay under tow with about seventy midshipmen of the U.S. Naval Academy on board. Anxious that Confederate troops might invade Maryland, the navy had moved the academy from Annapolis to Newport—specifically, to Fort Adams. The academy set up inside the fort and continued its program of preparing the midshipmen to be naval officers. Unfortunately, the young navy men found the fort too much of a temptation toward mischief, and in September, their professors decided to move them again, this time to the Atlantic House Hotel in the downtown Newport area, at the corner of Pelham Street and Bellevue Avenue.[51]

At the First Battle of Bull Run (First Manassas) on July 21, 1861, Colonel John S. Slocum, formerly a captain in the Ninth Rhode Island Infantry, which had trained at Fort Adams and fought in the Battle of Chapultepec, was struck down while commanding his troops in combat,

View of Fort Adams's northwest bastion during the Civil War. Note the shot furnace to the right of the tree. *National Archives/Daniel P. Titus Collection.*

reminiscent of the fate of his own former colonel in the Ninth, Truman B. Ransom.

From October 1862 until the end of the war, Fort Adams served as the headquarters of the Fifteenth Infantry Regiment of the regular army, under the command of Colonel Oliver L. Shepherd. Similar to the fort's role during the Mexican-American War less than twenty years earlier, the post became a recruit depot, where new enlistees reported for induction into the Union army; to receive their uniforms, weapons and other equipment; and to be sent to join the units of the regiment already deployed in the Southern states. The Fifteenth was one of nine "super regiments" authorized by Congress in 1861. These regiments were much larger than the standard regiments, which had ten companies and a total strength of about 1,000 men. In comparison, the "super regiments" had twenty-four companies organized into three eight-company battalions, for a total strength of about 2,400—just the number of troops Fort Adams had originally been designed and built to support. As each of these three battalions was almost as large as a regular regiment, they could operate independently of one another.

The entire "super regiment" of the Fifteenth could not be mobilized at the same time, however, so individual companies of about one hundred men each were organized at Fort Adams. The *Newport Mercury* recorded companies being shipped out to the front in three increments, on August 1 and 20, 1864, and on May 10, 1865. But in addition to serving as a deployment site, Fort Adams was also a place of retreat and rest. On June 17, 1865, while troops of the Fifteenth were still being mobilized to move out from the fort, their own First Battalion was ordered to return to Fort Adams from the field of battle. This battalion had been organized early in the war and was ordered to rest after seeing too much action at the front.

Fort Adams's (In)Famous General: Ambrose Burnside

In the 1840s, a man who would play a significant role in the Civil War was stationed at Fort Adams: Ambrose Burnside. Burnside was born in 1824 in Liberty, Indiana; entered West Point as a cadet on July 1, 1843; and graduated as a second lieutenant in the artillery on July 1, 1847. Among his classmates was a future commander of Fort Adams, Clermont Best, as well as future Confederate general A.P. Hill. Because Burnside graduated during the Mexican-American War, he soon found himself serving at recently captured Mexico City until October 1848, when he was transferred to Fort Adams with the Third Artillery Regiment.

During his time at Fort Adams, Burnside probably lived in one of the casemate officers' quarters on the southern end of the fort's east wall, as these quarters were arranged by rank, with the higher-ranked men at the wall's north end and then ranks declining toward the south. These east wall living quarters—though aesthetically ornate with decorated plaster walls, mouldings, fireplaces, ceiling rosettes and pocket doors—were also at that time damp and unhealthy, havens for mold and mildew. Dutch ovens were provided so officers could dine in their quarters with their families; enlisted men typically employed the larger "community" ovens in the southwest demi-bastion (remains of which can still be seen today). Water was chiefly provided by numerous cisterns, which collected rainwater through a system of flashing and lead pipes on the fort's rooftops.[52]

In 1849, however, Burnside departed Fort Adams for frontier duty at Las Vegas, then part of New Mexico, and sustained combat wounds during a skirmish with Jicarilla Apache there on August 23, 1849. After this posting, Burnside served in the garrison at Jefferson Barracks near St. Louis, Missouri, from 1850 to 1851. It was during this assignment, in December 1851, that Burnside was promoted to first lieutenant. Four months later, he began serving with the Mexican Boundary Commission, a position he held for nearly a year. In 1852, though, Burnside found himself once again serving at Fort Adams, and in this same year, he married Mary Richmond Bishop of Providence, Rhode Island. Burnside would continue at Fort Adams until his resignation from the army on October 2, 1853.

In his new life as a civilian, Burnside remained in Rhode Island but moved from Newport to Bristol, across Mount Hope Bay on the mainland, where he established a rifle manufacturing business in 1853. After only three years, he invented the "Burnside Breech-loading Carbine," a weapon designed and crafted for ease and rapidity of reload by cavalrymen on horseback. Unfortunately for Burnside, his company went out of business in 1858 due to petty politics. Secretary of War John Floyd, an ardent Democrat, ensured that the Republican Burnside's army contracts were canceled. As a result, Burnside was forced to liquidate the company and sell his patents to other manufacturers. Ironically, the army purchased about forty-five thousand Burnside carbines during the Civil War, but Burnside himself did not financially benefit from a single one of those purchases.

After the disappointment of his business failure, Burnside found employment with the railroad as cashier of the Land Department in 1858 with help of fellow West Point graduate and future general George B. McClellan, who was then vice-president of the Illinois Central Railroad. Burnside was promoted to treasurer of the company in 1860. While working for the Illinois Central, he made an acquaintance that would later prove consequential not only for his own life but also for the fortunes of the Union forces in the Civil War: future president Abraham Lincoln, then the railroad's general counsel.

With the outbreak of the Civil War, Burnside was appointed by Rhode Island governor William Sprague as colonel of the First Rhode

Island Detached Militia, and he served as a brigade commander at the First Battle of Bull Run on July 21. Along with his regiment, he was mustered out of volunteer service on August 2. Four days later, though, he was appointed as brigadier general of Volunteers and commanded a provisional brigade in the vicinity of Washington, D.C., from September 3 to October 23. The reason for Burnside's rapid rise may have been due to his being one of the few West Point graduates with ties to Rhode Island. As he was also one of the few senior officers in the army at the beginning of the Civil War, his seniority ensured that he would be considered for higher positions.

Burnside's next major assignment was the organization of the Coast Division of the Army of the Potomac at Annapolis from October 23, 1861, to January 8, 1862. Beginning on January 13, he was placed in command of the Department of North Carolina. In this capacity, throughout the remainder of the winter and into the early spring of 1862, Burnside commanded what would be known as the "Burnside Expedition," the goal of which was to capture key locations along to the coast of North Carolina to cut off Confederate trade with Europe, as well as provide potential bases for Union operations. The expedition engaged in the battle and capture of Roanoke Island (February 7–8), the attack on New Bern (March 16), the attack on Camden (April 19) and finally the bombardment of Fort Macon, resulting in its capture on April 26, 1862. As a result of this success, Burnside was widely considered one of the best generals in the Union army and was accordingly promoted to major general in the U.S. Volunteers.

Following this promotion, Burnside was reassigned to command the Ninth Corps of the Army of the Potomac, and it was this assignment that brought him to the Battle of Antietam on September 17, 1862—the bloodiest single day of the entire Civil War. Burnside's rising star began to plummet as a result of poor calculations and misjudgments, beginning with his conducting a frontal assault against a ferocious Confederate defense on a bridge over Antietam Creek, thereafter known infamously as "Burnside's Bridge." With the Union on one bank of the creek and the Confederates on the other, Burnside insisted that his forces funnel along the bridge to conduct this assault—a time-consuming effort that bottlenecked the Union troops. Although Burnside's corps eventually succeeded in crossing the creek, the success was short-lived, as a fresh Confederate division, ironically commanded by Burnside's West Point classmate A.P. Hill, arrived and forced Burnside to retreat. When it was later discovered that there was a nearby ford that could have been used to cross the creek much earlier, a saying arose that Burnside had a talent for "snatching defeat from the jaws of victory." Had Burnside used this ford, he could have flanked the Confederates, and the battle may have ended in a decisive Union victory rather than ending in an essential "draw."

Arguably, Burnside rose to the level of incompetence often attributed to him when he was appointed as commander of the Army of the Potomac on November 10, 1862, following the relief from command of his friend, Major General George McClellan. Burnside had twice previously turned down this very assignment on the grounds that he was unsuited to command a force of such great size, but now he accepted the position with reluctance. After Antietam, he achieved a further degree of infamy for his performance at the Battle of Fredericksburg on December 13, 1862, when he failed to move his troops quickly enough to prevent Confederate positions from being reinforced. Once in position, he delayed in making use of a pontoon bridge to cross the swollen Rappahannock River, deciding instead to wait for the full number of pontoons to arrive. This bought the Confederates time to further fortify the very positions Burnside was planning to attack. He decided to attack them anyway—a tactic that naturally resulted in heavy casualties without significant results.

Burnside was relieved from command of the Army of the Potomac on January 26, 1863, but he was reassigned to command of the Department of the Ohio. Here, Burnside generated some controversy when he arrested and court-martialed an Ohio Democrat congressman who was initially sentenced to prison but was banished to the Confederacy instead. Redeeming himself to a certain degree from his recent past errors, Burnside led the pursuit and capture of Morgan's Raiders in July and August, captured Cumberland Gap in September and participated in the Siege of Knoxville, Tennessee, from November 17 to December 1, 1863.

Burnside then moved east once again and resumed command of the Ninth Corps, which he led in a number of key operations in Virginia, including the Richmond Campaign; the Battle of the Wilderness on May 6, 1864; the Battle of Spotsylvania on May 9–12, 1864; and the Siege of Petersburg. It was during the latter siege that Burnside committed his final military blunder.

The commander of a Union regiment composed of Pennsylvania miners suggested tunneling under the Confederate lines and then detonating eight thousand pounds of gunpowder with the intent of blowing a large gap in the lines that could then be easily and quickly exploited. This was, in fact, a common tactic, known as a mining attack, and it had been employed since the Middle Ages. Heeding the regimental commander's advice, the tunnels were created and the explosion detonated on July 30, 1864. All went according to plan; it was the aftermath that sealed Burnside's reputation as a poor commander. Originally, Burnside had detailed a division of African American soldiers to lead the assault after the explosion, but shortly before the attack began, he received orders from his superior, Major General George Meade, to replace these soldiers with a white division. Burnside followed these orders, but whereas the African American soldiers had been specially trained for the mission, the white soldiers had not. As a result, they did not successfully exploit the weakness in the Confederate defenses, allowing the Confederates to rally and prevent the Union forces from breaking through their lines. The Union effort ended up being a spectacular failure.

As a result of this incident, known as the "crater debacle," Union army commander Ulysses S. Grant lost all confidence in Burnside as a field commander. On August 13, 1864, Grant issued Burnside orders to return to Rhode Island to await further orders, although these second orders never came. Burnside waited at Fort Adams until April 15, 1865, six days after Confederate general Robert E. Lee's surrender at Appomattox. Burnside then accepted that he would be of no further use to the army and submitted his final resignation.

Returning to civilian life once again, Burnside worked as a civil engineer and held various offices with several companies in the railroad industry. He later turned to politics and was elected governor of Rhode Island from May 1866 to May 1869. As governor, he personally signed certificates for every Rhode Island Civil War veteran as a means of both acknowledging and documenting their wartime service.

It certainly seems that Burnside was a far more able statesman than military commander. After his tenure as governor, he visited Europe in 1870 and was an observer of the Franco-Prussian War. He was admitted within the German and French lines in and around Paris, acting as a mediator in the peace negotiations between the two sides. He later returned to Rhode Island and was elected by the state Senate to serve as a United States senator, taking office on March 4, 1875, and being reelected in 1881. He died at his home in Bristol on September 13, 1881, at the age of fifty-seven and was buried at Providence's Swan Point Cemetery.

The End of the War

In December 1863, about five months after the decisive Battle of Gettysburg, Lieutenant Colonel Hoffman of the Sixth Infantry inspected Fort Adams to determine whether it might be suitable to accommodate Confederate prisoners of war. The lieutenant colonel found that the fort could hold up to six hundred prisoners, but Fort Warren, on George's Island in Boston Harbor, was ultimately chosen for the purpose instead.

After the war's end, on March 4, 1865—coinciding with the date of President Abraham Lincoln's second inauguration—Newport held a parade to honor the Union victories. Fittingly, the Fifteenth Infantry band from Fort Adams provided music for the occasion. But a little more than a month later, Fort Adams's troops participated in very different ceremonies: Newport observed Wednesday, April 19, as a day of mourning for the slain President Lincoln while his funeral was conducted in Washington. A memorial service was held at Fort Adams, and the men fired a twenty-one-gun salute in Lincoln's honor.

Fort Adams returned to its primary function as a major coastal artillery fort after 1865. Although the number of troops stationed there varied, especially according to whether the nation was at war or in peace, the fort typically had a regimental headquarters responsible for all coastal fortifications in New England, and its commanding officer was usually a colonel. Periodically, the garrison would be rotated between the coast and the western frontier, as those two tasks were the primary assignments for artillery units of this era. The former duty was as easy as the latter was hard, so the army's rotation policy was arranged not only to reward the efforts of those who had served in the unforgiving western states and territories but also to prevent the coastal garrisons from becoming too complacent.

But the methods and technology of warfare had advanced and changed considerably since the fort had first been designed in the early 1820s. Iron-plated battleships had been developed during the Civil War,

THE WARS OF THE NINETEENTH CENTURY

Late nineteenth-century view of a gun crew with a Civil War–era vintage 3-inch ordnance rifle. *John S. and Margaret D. Dugan Collection.*

making the old round cannon shot ineffective against naval attack. In December 1866, extensive alterations were made to the fort's west curtain in order to accommodate the emplacement of fifteen Rodman guns, then the state-of-the-art form of artillery whose pointed missiles could shear through the armor of the newly developed war vessels; the Rodman's rifled barrel also ensured greater accuracy and a longer range than the old smoothbore cannons had been capable of.

Favorite Daughter

The age of the Civil War and its aftermath was also the heyday of one of the country's handful of female lighthouse keepers, a figure who remains to this day in Newport's collective memory as one of the city's most beloved citizens. Ida Lewis, born in 1842, learned the trade of tending Lime Rock Lighthouse from her father, Hosea. When Ida was only sixteen years old, her father suffered a crippling stroke, and the daily responsibility of keeping the light clean and burning into the dark nights over Newport Harbor fell to his teenage daughter.

When Hosea died, Ida was officially commissioned as Lime Rock Lighthouse keeper. But she would go much further than simply keeping the lenses clean, making sure the oil never ran out and waking at all hours to care for the light in a habit she compared to a mother knowing when her child needed her in the dead of night.[53] During the half century that she tended the light, she would become renowned and honored throughout the nation for the courage she displayed in taking her little skiff onto dangerous waters in terrifying weather conditions in order to rescue unfortunate souls whose vessels had capsized in the waters of Newport Harbor. Overall, Lewis was credited with rescuing eighteen people—and that was merely the official count.[54] The actual count was possibly higher.

Being a close neighbor of Miss Lewis, just a short way across the water from Lime Rock, Fort Adams naturally developed a fairly close association with the local heroine. Throughout the fort's history, the men of the garrison frequently enjoyed leave in town by boating back and forth across the harbor, and on some occasions they met with calamity on the trip. In 1842—the year of Ida Lewis's birth—two artillerymen by the names of Brown and Bush drowned when their sailboat capsized in the harbor.[55] We can only guess how many Fort Adams soldiers were grateful when Ida grew up and began her duties at Lime Rock.

On one occasion in April 1869, the seemingly fearless lighthouse keeper saved the lives of one Sergeant Adams and his friend Private McLaughlin when the boat they were traveling in had a mishap in the middle of the harbor. To express their gratitude, the men of the fort presented Lewis a reward of $218 two months later. Lewis would again come to the aid of two soldiers on February 4, 1881. This time, the inebriated victims committed the unthinkable foolishness of attempting to walk across the "frozen" harbor on their return to the fort after a day in town. Ida Lewis spotted them from a kitchen window of the lighthouse and watched as both men crashed through the unstable ice. Without a moment's hesitation, Lewis hiked up her skirts and ran to the men's aid, herself venturing out onto ice that she well knew to be treacherous. Incredibly, she literally reeled them both in with a length of clothesline, nearly losing her own life when the panicking soldiers pulled so hard on the line that Lewis too fell forward and through the ice, her heavy, layered nineteenth-century clothing dragging her down in the arctic water. But through sheer grit, steely nerve and force of will, she pulled herself out and finally succeeded in hauling both men to safety. As a direct result of this act of raw heroism, Congress recognized Lewis's mettle on July 16 of that same year with the granting of the Gold Lifesaving Medal, First Class.

In May 1892, Ida Lewis would once again appear on the scene when a group of Fort Adams soldiers was in danger. But this time, one would be beyond her reach. At nine o'clock on the night of Sunday, May 22, artillerymen William Sheehan, Walter L. Ford, Harry C. Davis, William H. Hathaway and Thomas Moulton were crossing Newport Harbor in Sheehan's sailboat, heading back to the fort from town. The *Newport Daily News* for Monday, May 23, reported that "[e]very one in the boat was sober, but they evidently were not skilled boatmen." Perhaps the darkness of the night compounded their error.

Before the men reached the fort, the boat capsized, pitching all of its occupants into the water. Three of them made for Goat Island, Fort Adams's neighbor across the harbor—Ford and Moulton reached the safety of the Newport Harbor Light, and Hathaway reached the island's torpedo station. That left Davis and Sheehan still in the water. Amid the shouting of the men, the confusion of the darkness and the pull of the waves, the sound of gunfire rang out—it was the indomitable Ida Lewis, firing shots into the air from Lime Rock to let the men would know which direction led to safety. One wonders why she didn't row out to them as she'd done so often before. Perhaps she'd seen them too late and knew that there was no chance for her to reach them in time, or perhaps she was in the midst of tending the light and couldn't leave her task. Giving them a signal, trying to show them the way, was the best she could do in that moment.

But Sheehan knew that he wasn't going to make it. One of his friends—probably Davis—vowed to stay by his side until they were rescued, but Sheehan refused to allow his friend to risk his life. The drowning man warned that if Davis didn't save himself, he was sure to go down as well, and Sheehan outright told Davis to leave him to his fate lest two lives be lost rather than one. Davis obeyed and swam for a rescuing boat, while Sheehan was pulled to his death by the water, all the while screaming, "Help me! Help me! For God's sake!" But by that time, Davis himself was far off, fighting for his own life, and couldn't answer his friend's desperate plea.

Gravestone of Ida Lewis at the historic Newport Common Burying Ground. A detail of Fort Adams soldiers assisted at her funeral. *Kathleen Troost-Cramer.*

Meanwhile, a man named Christian Luth had heard the men's cries and launched his skiff from the Newport docks to help them. He found Ford and Moulton first and took them into the small boat, and then he made for Davis, "who was going down for the last time, and he seized the drowning man by the hair and, with the aid of the other two, pulled him into the boat in an exhausted condition." The three men were then transferred to a fishing schooner, the *Harry and Harvey*, which brought them to the safety of the city's wharves, while the Goat Island torpedo station's launch brought Hathaway in. All four survivors spent the night at the Newport police station under observation for their health and returned to the fort by ambulance the next day. Sheehan's body was recovered and interred at the Fort Adams cemetery, where his grave can be seen to this day.[56]

So grateful were the men of Fort Adams for Miss Lewis's help over the years that a detail from the fort accompanied her remains to the place of her burial in the Newport Common Burying Ground when she was laid to rest in October 1911.

After the War: A New Role

In the decade following the Civil War, Fort Adams was graced by the presence of several colorful personalities. The first of these was one Thomas W. Sherman (often referred to as "the Other Sherman" to distinguish him from the more famous Union general known chiefly for his "March to the Sea" and the burning of Atlanta). Sherman was a Newport native who had served with distinction in the southern theater of war and had been so grievously wounded at Port Hudson, Louisiana, that the *Newport Daily News* mistakenly published his obituary. Although he survived, one of his legs was amputated above the knee—an all-too-common result of being struck by the savage weaponry employed during the Civil War. Despite this loss of limb, Sherman remained in active service and went on to command Fort Adams from 1866 to 1869.[57]

On the day that rang in the new year of 1800, a French immigrant named E.I. DuPont arrived in Newport. Just four years later, he negotiated his first business contract in his adopted country—as supplier of gunpowder to both army and navy of the United States. His company would go on to be the primary gunpowder supplier to the Union forces throughout the Civil War. The successful industrialist's grandson, Henry A. DuPont, enrolled in the military academy at West Point and finished his career there by graduating at the top of his class. A commission in the Fifth Artillery Regiment followed, and the younger DuPont went on to serve with distinction in the Battles of Opequan, Fisher's Hill and Cedar Creek. As a result of these battlefield honors, DuPont was promoted to captain and awarded not one but two brevet (that is, honorary) ranks to major and lieutenant colonel. The celebrated DuPont was later assigned to command the light artillery at Fort Adams from July 1870 to September 1873. The proverbial wheel of time had turned—in two generations, the grandson of the first DuPont had returned to the city that had first welcomed his grandfather to its shores—and chances are good that at least a few of the gunpowder kegs at Fort Adams already bore the DuPont family name when the colonel arrived.

DuPont's tenure at Fort Adams was short-lived, however. In 1875, he resigned from the army to take his place in the family business—finding even greater success than his military career had brought him. Two short years after leaving the service, he became president of the Wilmington & Northern Railroad, and he went on to serve as senator from Delaware from 1906 to 1917.

But recognition for his battle prowess was a long time in coming. It wasn't until 1898 that DuPont was finally awarded the Medal of Honor for combat valor at the 1864 Battle of Cedar Creek.[58]

In the year of DuPont's resignation from the army, another future Medal of Honor recipient was stationed at Fort Adams. George Uhri, an artillery sergeant, enlisted in Battery F, Fifth U.S. Artillery Regiment, in 1858. At White Oak Swamp in Virginia, on June 30, 1862, Uhri, with two comrades, took the initiative without waiting for orders to take over an abandoned field gun from a neighboring Union battery. The three men saved the piece from falling into enemy hands while the Confederates advanced and poured on the firepower. Uhri earned his Medal of Honor that day but, like DuPont, had to wait more than thirty years for his official recognition; the award wasn't granted until 1898. Uhri continued in the army after the war, serving faithfully until his retirement on December 31, 1886. He died in New York City in 1911.

The army's nineteenth-century policy of rotating units between various posts meant that it was not uncommon for a soldier to serve his entire military career in one regiment, if not the same company. Due to these rotations, the troops stationed at Fort Adams would change every few years. In 1870, a company of artillerymen was rotated to Fort Adams from Fort Warren in Boston Harbor. On September 27, 1870, the *Newport Mercury* reported that these soldiers' behavior on town leave was so disgraceful that "[s]ome of them appear to forget that they are among civilized people." The same article then expressed confidence that the fort's commanding officer would deal most effectively with the situation.

In early November 1870, 250 troops from Fort Adams, composing three companies of artillerymen and one light battery, were sent to New York to "regulate" that city's election. As New York was noted for volatile politics that could often turn violent in the nineteenth century, an acute need was felt to have soldiers in the city in the event that things got out of hand. The notorious draft riots of July 1863 in which hundreds of people were killed were still fresh in the minds of most Americans seven years later. Fortunately, though, there were no disturbances this time, and the troops returned to Fort Adams in just two days.

On Fort Adams's birthday, July 4, 1877, a bizarre accident occurred reminiscent of the fate of Jennie Wade, the only civilian killed during the Battle of Gettysburg. While staying with her sister, whose house sat in the no-man's-land between encamped Union and Confederate troops, Union sympathizer Miss Wade went into her sister's kitchen one morning to make bread for the Union troops stationed beyond the house's back door. A rogue shot from a Rebel musket penetrated two doors to strike Jennie in the back, and she died instantly. To this day, no one knows where that fatal shot came from, but in Fort Adams's "sister case" to this incident, the identity of the shooter *is* known.

Across the bay's East Passage, at Jamestown, a young Newport resident named Minnie Howard was enjoying a picnic with friends from her congregation at Zion Church.[59] At about three o'clock in the afternoon, while standing with a friend at the rocky outcropping known as the Dumplings and looking across the bay toward Fort Adams, Miss Howard commented, "What a pleasant sail we shall have home."[60] Just then, though, the attention of the two women was caught by a splash below them—a bullet fired from the fort had struck the water only feet away. Stunned, someone in the party noted with anger and alarm how irresponsible it was for soldiers to shoot toward a place where people were known to live and take recreation.

It wasn't the first time a serious accident had befallen Jamestown as a result of training at Fort Adams. Two years earlier, in October 1875, authorized target practice by the Fifth Artillery resulted in a cannon shot overreaching its target, traveling into Jamestown and "coming within about four feet of a farmer's head passing through the body of a cow and imbed[ing] itself in the soil."[61]

Practically before Miss Howard's friend had finished her diatribe on the soldiers' carelessness, another shot rang out from the fort. Miss Howard staggered; this bullet had struck high in her chest and exited through her right shoulder. It was a potentially fatal wound, and action had to be taken quickly. Fortunately, another group of picnickers nearby included some doctors, who immediately answered the frantic cries for help. These men managed to stem the flow of blood from Miss Howard's wound while awaiting a way to safely get her to a location where she could receive real treatment. Help soon arrived from all quarters: a doctor named Enge traveled from downtown Newport, and the Naval Torpedo Station on Goat Island sent a launch that took Miss Howard back to the city. A stretcher was waiting at Ferry Wharf to carry her to her home at the Perry House, and there more doctors arrived to attempt to save her life.

Although the shot had definitely come from Fort Adams, the culprits were not apprehended right away, since they had, of course, run from the spot when they realized what their actions had caused. But they could not hide for long—very quickly, investigation revealed the story. The day after the shooting, three soldiers informed their superior officer that they had decided to "celebrate" the anniversary of the nation's independence by firing a musket in the direction of Fort Dumplings. They came to this decision entirely on their own and had not received authorization to fire any weapon. One of the men, Private Heins, fired two shots that fell into the water, one of which was the bullet Miss Howard and her friend had heard fall just short of where they were standing.

The next man to take a turn with the weapon was Private Selmer Grimm, and it was his shot that had inadvertently found a human target. Grimm was no green recruit, though: he was a seasoned veteran with close to thirty years' service to his credit. But a time-honored tradition at Fort Adams was to give the soldiers an extra ration of liquor on July 4 in celebration of the nation's independence, as well as the original Fort Adams's commissioning in 1799. One can only speculate, but it would not be beyond possibility that Grimm and his two comrades had been drinking too much and that their judgment was accordingly impaired. Whatever the case, the men were court-martialed and sentenced to one month in the fort stockade and the loss of one month's pay. Due to the men's remorse over the incident and cooperation with the investigation, however, there was a doubt as to whether this full sentence would be carried out or lessened to some degree.

Fortunately for Minnie Howard, the piercing of her body by the wayward musket ball did not prove fatal. The efforts of her friends and physicians to save her life were successful, and on July 13, a little more than a week after she had been wounded, the *Newport Daily News* reported an excellent prognosis for her full recovery.

"Battle" Tested

One of the most popular spectacles to occur periodically at Fort Adams was an occasional mock battle, often referred to in newspaper accounts as a "sham attack." In these war games, the U.S. Navy would enter the East Passage of Narragansett Bay and "attack" the fort, which the artillerymen would valiantly "defend." Two such encounters took place in October and November 1877. Little known to anyone at the time, these exercises would prove to be the precursor to Joint Operations, so integral to the warfare technology and techniques of the twentieth century.

These occasions, which would continue until the period of the Second World War, were quite the spectacle. On one occasion in 1887, the *Newport Daily News* repeated a report that had appeared in the *Fall River Globe* that the noise of the artillery from both sides in these exercises could be heard clearly in neighboring Portsmouth, across the Sakonnet River in Tiverton, and even as far away as the capital city of Providence.[62]

Although Fort Adams was ready for action, authorities began to note even as early as the outbreak of the Civil War that the fort was falling into disrepair and that it might prove unable to stand against the rapidly advancing technology of battle. In 1868, Congress granted $150,000 for the fort's repair, especially for extensive work on the west curtain.[63] One year later, the *Newport Mercury* reported that the fort was still undergoing renovations expressly "to make it

A 15-inch Rodman gun fires on a U.S. Navy squadron during a joint army-navy exercise circa 1884. *John S. and Margaret D. Dugan Collection.*

View of Brenton Cove from the Beacon Rock estate. Note the mule stables and mules on the right. *Fort Adams Trust.*

strong enough to withstand the concussion of the 15-inch guns that are now being placed on the fortifications of the country."[64] But again in 1868, that same paper noted that work had stopped until it could be shown that Fort Adams was still capable of providing a viable defense against the emerging tactics of battle. "Upon all old fortifications work is to cease until it is ascertained what kind of material can be found capable of resisting the ponderous shots thrown by the modern guns," the *Newport Mercury* reported in December 1868. "Works like Fort Adams would offer but little resistance to a fleet of Monitors with heavy equipment.[65]

At the time this comment was made, Fort Adams in its completed state was only eleven years old.

The Spanish-American War and the End of the Nineteenth Century

In 1898, during the Spanish-American War, Fort Adams was brought into a high state of readiness in the event of an attack on Newport. Although these fears turned out to be unfounded, the fort was used as a training base by eighty members of the Newport Artillery Company for one week when the men came to the fort to practice firing the massive fifteen-inch Rodman guns, which had replaced the old smoothbore cannons. The fort also hosted a National Guard regiment from New York for some time while the men were waiting to be deployed to the theater of war.

As the new century approached, attention turned to improving the living conditions of the soldiers stationed at the fort. Prior to this time, most soldiers were quartered in the casemates along the fort's southeast and southwest walls. Along with the addition of new brick

Late 1800s view of west wall interior ditch. Note the cannons and piles of cannonballs lined up along the ditch. *John S. and Margaret D. Dugan Collection.*

Fort Adams

View of east and southeast walls in the early twentieth century. *National Archives/Daniel P. Titus Collection.*

Southeast wall of Fort Adams during the late 1800s. Note the "mud rooms" in front of the entrances to the casemates. *National Archives/Daniel P. Titus Collection.*

barracks, the casemates of the south walls below were converted into mess halls, kitchens, showers, latrines and offices. Nor were these the only improvements to the fort at this time: the bakery, formerly located in the southeast demi-bastion, was moved to its own building north of the fort's east gate, and a new stockade (army parlance for "jail") was built just to the south of the new bakery. (Perhaps this proximity was an intentional punishment for the soldiers incarcerated in the stockade's cells, knowing that these insubordinate men would catch the mouthwatering aromas wafting from the bakery!) Also at this time, the old cisterns were replaced by indoor plumbing, and telephone lines and electric wiring brought the fort into the early twentieth century.

From the late 1800s to 1917, an era of fortification adaptation known as the Endicott Period, several modern gun batteries were installed beyond the fort's southern walls. Naval warfare had advanced to the stage where a battleship's guns could tear down the granite of

Southeast wall as viewed from parade ground. Note the platform for physical training instruction at left. *John S. and Margaret D. Dugan Collection.*

The Wars of the Nineteenth Century

Above: Broad jump competition on the parade field, early twentieth century. *John S. and Margaret D. Dugan Collection.*

Opposite: A 12-inch mortar firing. Note the casual pose of the soldier on the right as the projectile exits the barrel. *National Archives/Daniel P. Titus Collection.*

the great west curtain, formerly the deadliest part of the fort enemy vessels had to cross. The west wall was no longer a feasible defensive location but rather a vulnerable target. The guns were removed. From now on, Newport Harbor's defense would rely on five state-of-the-art artillery emplacements lined up along the approach to Narragansett Bay. These batteries complemented several others of the same period in Rhode Island and formed the primary coastal defense installations

Soldiers in front of guardhouse near the east gate, circa 1890s. *John S. and Margaret D. Dugan Collection.*

until the outbreak of World War II in 1939. For the next several decades, the fort's stone perimeter was only used as the primary housing for enlisted personnel, with barracks for junior soldiers located in brick dormitories constructed along the fort's southeast and southwest walls in 1906 and 1908, respectively. Noncommissioned officers were housed in the former officers' quarters in the east wall and in the area around the northwest bastion. With the new batteries, Fort Adams's defenses were more than a match for any warship afloat at that time.

This meant that after 1904, there was now an abundance of empty, underutilized or completely unused space in the west wall. Army ingenuity went to work to create structures for the use of the community, especially taking into consideration tired soldiers coming off a long day of hard training: part of the wall's center tier, formerly built to equip armaments to spray enemy vessels' decks with grapeshot, was converted into an enlisted men's club (known as the taproom), a small movie theater and the base post office. Below, in the tier designed to house guns that would blast through wooden hulls in the early 1800s, a boiler room, library, recreational shooting range for .22-caliber rifles and two-lane bowling alley were installed. The latter feature was "staffed" by young boys living at the fort, employed as pin setters at two cents per string.

PART III
THE WARS TO END ALL WARS

The First World War

In September 1902, another war game was held by a joint effort of the army and navy, involving ships of the Atlantic fleet and the range of forts protecting Narragansett Bay. The attacking fleet was commanded by Admiral Higginson, who used the battleship *Kearsarge* as his flagship. The significance of this exercise lay in the fact that it was one of the few peacetime cooperative efforts between army and navy prior to the late twentieth century. It also provided an opportunity for the new batteries to be tested under realistic circumstances.

The secretary of war from 1900 to 1905, a man named Elihu Root, was arguably the most innovative individual in history to hold this high position. He distinguished himself in the office by advocating greater cooperation between the branches of the armed forces and believed strongly in making practical use of the National Guard as a ready reserve to augment the regular army in time of war. After Root left office, his legacy was directly responsible for a new program: stationing National Guard troops to man coastal fortifications. Rhode Island was considered the perfect location for a trial run of this concept, as the state's maritime location and heavy fortifications already in place offered an ideal stage.

Soldiers in barracks, pre–World War I. This photo was possibly taken in the now-demolished light artillery battery barracks. *National Archives/Daniel P. Titus Collection.*

Because this new practice meant that National Guardsmen would naturally be integrated with regular army units for training,[66] Fort Adams began hosting National Guard regiments at this time. Within a few years, National Guard troops were redesignated as Coast Artillery units, and this assisted these troops in preparing for their actual mobilization mission of manning the state's coast defenses when the need arose in both world wars. However, the recognition that state militias should be organized and trained to man coastal fortifications in wartime was not new: presciently, Rhode Island militiaman Brevet Major Henry Cushing was assigned to evaluate his militia at its annual encampment in 1883. At that time, Cushing observed that the militia should be organized into heavy artillery troops for coastal defense. Perhaps Cushing's former assignment as a Fort Adams soldier had inspired this vision, but it would not be realized until nearly a quarter of a century after he gave it voice.

From July 7 through July 14, 1907, several companies of the Rhode Island National Guard trained at both Fort Adams and Fort Greble, another Coast Artillery fortification on Dutch Island, off the west side of Jamestown. At that time, the bulk of the Rhode Island National Guard was organized into First and Second Infantry Regiments, each with eight companies that possessed an authorized strength of three officers and forty-seven enlisted men. The First Regiment was sent to Fort Greble and the Second to Fort Adams. Each company was assigned to a regular army unit for training purposes, a significant arrangement that marked the first time Guardsmen would train on the modern artillery pieces equipping the fort's batteries.

The men devoted three full days—from Monday, July 8, to Wednesday, July 10, 1907—to instruction on the artillery pieces. The men were organized into reliefs to allow continuous training with no interruptions. This training included night drills in which boats would run in and out of the harbor, testing the effectiveness of Fort Adams's defenses. The same year also marked a major reorganization of the army's Artillery Corps: rather than have units for both field and seacoast duties in the same branch of service, the army separated the two into the Coast Artillery Corps and the Field Artillery Corps. The former was structured by numbered companies organized into districts until 1920, when regiments were formed. The largest effect of this reorganization, though, was an acknowledgement of significant differences between coast and field artillery.

This joint training continued in 1908 and 1909, but there were drastic changes in 1910. The well-to-do residents of Newport's famous summer colony—those families of the post–Civil War industrial boom responsible for the creation of the spectacularly opulent mansions lining Bellevue Avenue, most of which have not lost their power to drop jaws even today— began protesting vigorously that the firing of the large guns at both Fort Adams and Fort Wetherill was quite disturbing to them. As a result, Senator George Peabody Wetmore—himself a member of the same family who had constructed Newport's very first summer "cottage," Château-sur-Mer—addressed a letter dated June 13, 1910 to Mr. John T. Spencer, Esquire. The letter informed Mr. Spencer that there would be no firing of Forts Adams and Wetherill's guns with service (that is, full gunpowder) charges during the summer months. It is unfortunate indeed that so little appreciation was shown to the men guarding the very opportunity, freedom and ability of those summer colonists to enjoy the riches they had amassed.

Opposite, top: Soldiers lounge in upstairs barracks. *Fort Adams Trust.*

Opposite, bottom: Early twentieth-century view of upstairs barracks on top of the south walls of the fort. *John S. and Margaret D. Dugan Collection.*

Fort Adams

An ominous harbinger of things to come appeared with the arrival of German submarine *U-53* in Newport for a "diplomatic" visit on October 7, 1916. Under the guise of friendly gesture, this was actually a move intended to put the United States on notice that Germany had the capability, for the first time in history, of crossing the Atlantic undetected and reaching American shores—including important and strategic port cities with strong military presences. After the vessel's departure the very next morning, it attacked and sank five merchant ships in less than twenty-four hours. Needless to say, this incident provided impetus for the military to strengthen the defenses of Newport Harbor, including (and perhaps most especially) the Coast Artillery presence at Fort Adams.

When the United States entered the First World War in August 1917, twenty companies of Coast Artillery troops from the Rhode Island National Guard were activated to assist in reinforcing regular army troops stationed at coastal fortifications throughout the state of Rhode Island. Of these, fourteen companies were assigned to the Narragansett Bay forts, including Fort Adams. The remainder was sent to Boston and New Bedford. While Fort Adams continued its record of never seeing combat action for the entirety of the war, its function as a headquarters for all Rhode Island coastal defenses and a training base for units deployed to theaters of war in France was ultimately vital to the nation's war effort and success. Once in France, Coast Artillery soldiers were invaluable to American ground forces as the only men equipped to provide support with heavy artillery pieces ranging all the way up to fourteen-inch railway guns. Because the regulars were gone from the coastal forts at home, about half of the units assigned to Rhode Island forts were remobilized National Guardsmen, whose previous training with the regular army was now proving its worth.

Among the units formed at Fort Adams was the First Expeditionary Coast Artillery Brigade, under the command of Brigadier General George T. Bartlett. This brigade consisted of three Coast Artillery regiments.[67]

Opposite, top: Mess hall decorated for Christmas in 1911. *Fort Adams Trust.*

Opposite, bottom: Early twentieth-century view of exterior of post exchange, located in northwest bastion. *John S. and Margaret D. Dugan Collection.*

THE WARS TO END ALL WARS

In July 1918, Fort Adams was home to the Seventh Battalion of United States Guards—units made up of soldiers who, by reason of age or disability, were unsuited for frontline service and were instead assigned to provide security for military bases and defense plants.

At some point during the war, eight of Fort Adams's sixteen twelve-inch mortars were removed and sent to France for use as railway artillery. This was a common occurrence during World War I, as the army had discovered that having two mortars in a mortar pit was almost as effective as having the standard four, having the added attraction of making no additional manpower demands.

Fort Adams did not need to come under direct attack from German forces during World War I in order to experience fatalities. The deadliest enemy that invaded the fort in the fall of 1918 was the terrible epidemic of Spanish influenza, known to this day as one of the worst disease outbreaks in world history. In the United States alone, "the grip" was responsible for more than 600,000 deaths, with the state of Rhode Island experiencing between 2,000 and 3,000.

The flu arrived in Newport by way of the city's naval installations in August and spread rapidly and aggressively to the civilian population. Perhaps because of its remote location on Brenton's Point and its self-sufficient nature, Fort Adams was late in manifesting signs of this illness. The fort had initiated quarantine measures in late summer, but it wasn't until mid- to late September that deaths began to be recorded. Within a little less than a month, at least five soldiers had fallen to the flu, in addition to the infant daughter of Lieutenant Richard Geary, whose pregnant wife, Delia, went into early labor at Newport Hospital and gave birth to a baby girl. The premature birth caused the infant's death within moments, and Delia followed, her official cause of death described in the city record as "Broncho Pneumonia; Influenza; Childbirth."[68]

Opposite, top: Soldiers in a west wall casemate post exchange in the early twentieth century. Note the cold-weather clothing. *John S. and Margaret D. Dugan Collection.*

Opposite, bottom: Circa 1900 photo of a gun crew for a 12-inch mortar at Fort Adams. Soldiers were later provided with dungaree uniforms for working coast artillery pieces. The long pole is used for loading the projectile into the mortar and cleaning the bore. *John S. and Margaret D. Dugan Collection.*

The Fort Adams football team in 1924. *John S. and Margaret D. Dugan Collection.*

Fort Adams

Baseball practice on parade ground. *Fort Adams Trust.*

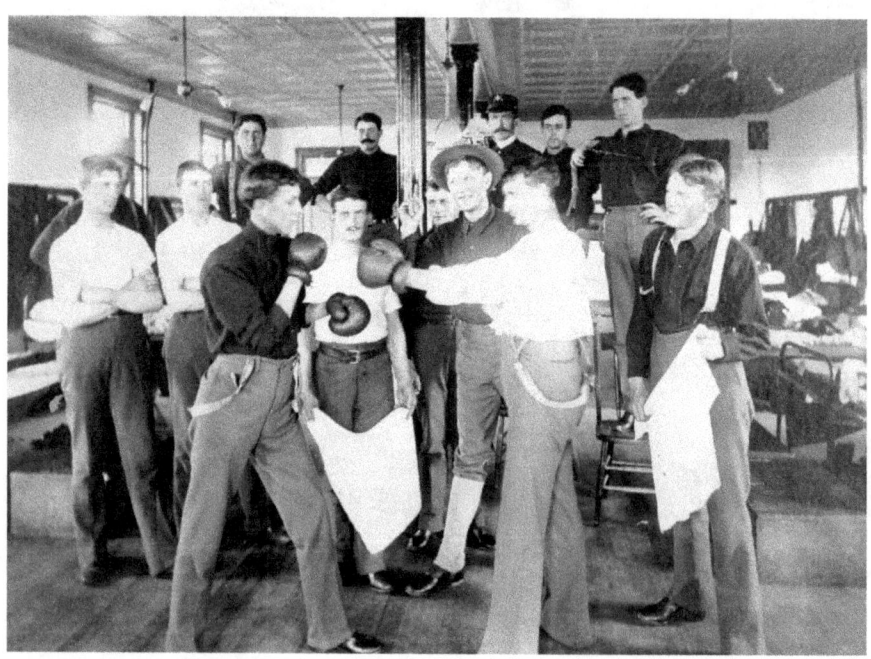

Soldiers practicing boxing stances in an upstairs barracks. *Fort Adams Trust.*

The Wars to End All Wars

On November 11, 1918, the armistice ending the First World War was signed. The National Guard units that had been activated for the duration of the war were demobilized in December, and smaller forts in the area were deactivated over the next three years. As of January 11, 1919, Fort Adams was garrisoned by five Coast Artillery companies, entering a period of peacetime complacency that would last more than two decades.

The post–World War I period was one of the best in Fort Adams's history. During this era, the soldiers lived a fairly easy life, while officers could look forward to completing their official duties by noon and spending the rest of the day riding or playing golf on the nine-hole short course near the southern boundary of the fort's reservation. It was during this time that Fort Adams earned a reputation as "the country club of the army,"[69] a fitting moniker for a military base that possessed as many recreational and leisure facilities as a small town, where troops could enjoy movie nights, visit the base library and dance the night away at socials organized by Fort Adams's own event organizer, Miss Maude Allen.

Soldiers and fort hostess Maude Allen near the post chapel during World War II. Miss Allen is buried at the fort's cemetery. *Fort Adams Trust.*

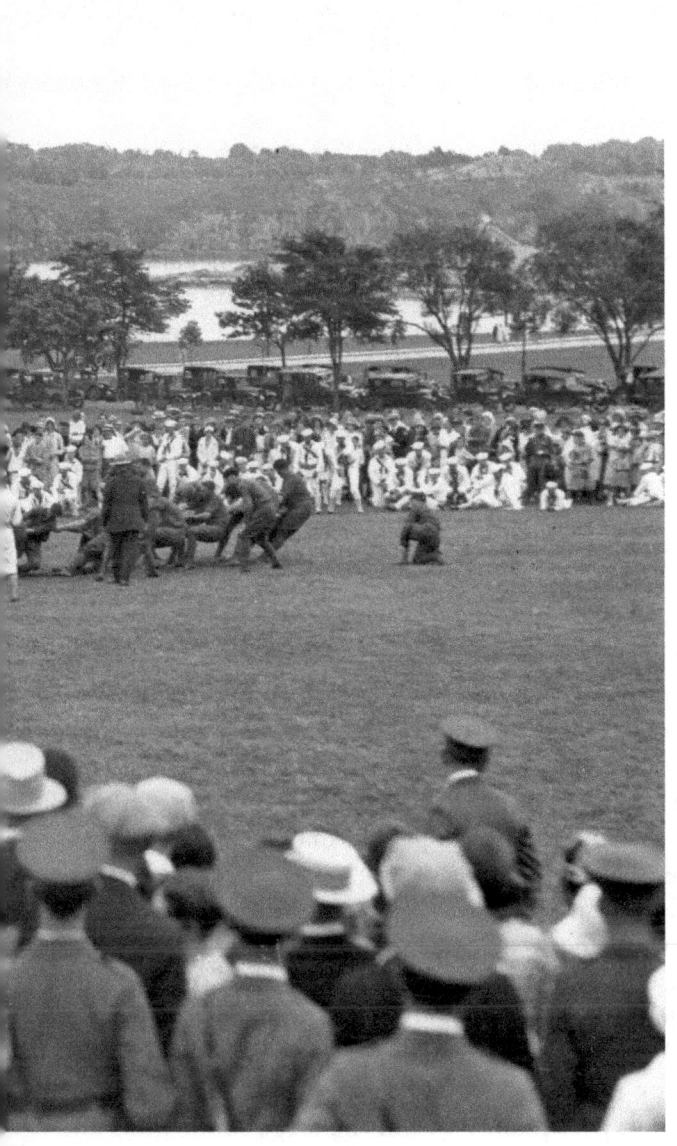

Soldiers and sailors engage in tug of war during a field day at Fort Adams in the early twentieth century. *John S. and Margaret D. Dugan Collection.*

Miss Allen began her job at the fort in about 1930, employed as official hostess of the service club; she would hold this job through the Second World War. In addition to her formal duties of managing the club, she also served as Fort Adams's unofficial ombudsman, bringing to the commanding officer's attention any complaints the soldiers could not resolve through the chain of command. "Maudie" was considered a part of the Fort Adams family, a well-loved personality around the fort community. She had her own quarters at the fort and lived there until her death in 1953, at which time her remains were carried to a grave in the fort cemetery by several retired sergeants who had served with her during her time at Fort Adams.

As was the lot of the entire Coast Artillery, the irony and perhaps frustration of preparing for a battle that would never be fought and waiting for fleets of attacking ships that would never come must have taken its toll without the outlets provided by Fort Adams's recreational pursuits.

During this time, Fort Adams was used as a training site by the Citizens' Military Training Camps (CMTC), starting in the summer of 1924. The CMTC program allowed young men to learn basic military skills without having to actually enlist in the army. The annual program took four weeks in the summer, usually in the month of July, over a total of four years, although relatively few stayed to complete the entire course, which would entitle them to an officer's commission. Ultimately, CMTC graduates provided an invaluable nucleus of trained soldiers around which combat-ready units could be organized and trained.

In 1922, a young lieutenant named Lyman G. Lemnitzer graduated from West Point. His first assignment was to Fort Adams as the base recreation and commissary officer. While this first posting was uneventful, Lemnitzer would go on to greatness, being promoted in 1955 to the rank of full "fourstar" general; from 1957 through to 1969, he would be assigned successively as army chief of staff, chairman of the Joint Chiefs of Staff and supreme Allied commander, Europe. Lemnitzer remains the only officer in American history to have been assigned to all three of the highest postings an army officer can occupy.

A particularly fascinating development and a truly forgotten— one may even say literally lost—piece of Fort Adams's history that occurred between the world wars was the commissioning of artists early in 1934 to create murals on the interior walls of the recreation facilities and mess halls, presumably within the fort's south walls and

Athletics on the parade ground. *National Archives/Daniel P. Titus Collection.*

The Fort Adams baseball team between the world wars. *Fort Adams Trust.*

Citizens Military Training Camps (CMTC) students work with the 12-inch mortars of Battery Greene in the summer of 1926. *John S. and Margaret D. Dugan Collection.*

perhaps of the interior west curtain as well.[70] Artwork for the Service Club was also anticipated. This was a joint effort between Fort Adams and the Rhode Island School of Design's R. Earl Rowe in support of the short-lived Civil Works Administration (CWA), a government initiative under Franklin D. Roosevelt's "New Deal" to create and sponsor work for the massive number of unemployed citizens still suffering the effects of the Great Depression. Ultimately deemed too financially burdensome, the CWA was dissolved in March 1934, but it proved to be the forerunner of Roosevelt's later (and more successful) Works Progress Administration.[71] Subjects for the Fort Adams murals were to include events in the history of Newport, as well as the famous Thirteenth Infantry that had been stationed at the fort. Apparently, though, the planned murals never became a reality—perhaps because the CWA ceased to exist only two months after the finalization of plans to host the artists. One can only imagine how the different the face of Fort Adams would look, even today, had those paintings ever taken form.

Late in 1938, six Fort Adams soldiers from the Thirteenth Infantry were awarded the Soldier's Medal, the highest commendation for noncombat heroism for rescuing a family from their home on Price's

The Wars to End All Wars

Soldiers being inspected in formation in about 1930. Note the laundry being air-dried hanging on railing of upstairs balcony. *National Archives/Daniel P. Titus Collection.*

Early twentieth-century view of a mess hall located in a lower-level casemate of either the southeast or southwest wall. *John S. and Margaret D. Dugan Collection.*

Neck in Newport during the terrible and infamous hurricane that struck on September 12 of that year. The Hurricane of 1938 remains one of the worst New England storms on record and was responsible for great loss of life.

THE SECOND WORLD WAR

With the outbreak of World War II, the United States began to mobilize and modernize its defenses. Just a few decades after their creation, the Endicott Period batteries were already obsolete. Six- and sixteen-inch guns mounted at Forts Varnum and Greene in Narragansett; at Fort Church in Little Compton, across the Sakonnet River to the north of Aquidneck Island; at Saunderstown's Fort Kearny; and at Fort Getty and Fort Wetherill, both on the southern end of Jamestown (known as "Beavertail"), now provided the main force of artillery in the Narragansett Bay area. Fort Adams's only guns from this time on were three-inch antiaircraft guns.

However, the fort was far from inactive, continuing to serve as the headquarters of the bay's harbor defenses. Attack from visible enemy vessels was no longer a threat; the chief seagoing terror now was the submarine—admittedly not new, but now greatly perfected by the German *Kriegsmarine*. To ward off Nazi U-boats, underwater mines were sown at all approaches to the bay, and in 1941, a steelcable anti-submarine net was installed between Forts Adams and Wetherill, as well as across the west passage on the west side of Jamestown.

It must be said that the closest thing to dangerous "action" that Fort Adams saw during this time was a dramatic water rescue on the night of July 14, 1941.[72] At about 9:30 p.m., a small group of Fort Adams soldiers caught sight of a flickering orange glow out in the East Passage. Every man knew that light could mean only one thing: fire. When they ran toward the shoreline to find its source, they saw a thirty-foot power cabin cruiser on the water nearly engulfed in flame. Worse, the soldiers recognized the cruiser: it belonged to none other than their own quartermaster, Lieutenant George L. Booth. The lieutenant was on board, striving to conquer the flames along with his companion, a Newport woman named Marion Boyle, but it was clear that the two

North gate of Fort Adams in about 1940. Note the sign with historic information about the Fort. *National Archives/Daniel P. Titus Collection.*

were fighting a losing battle as the fire devoured their vessel. In a matter of moments, the passengers would have to abandon the boat and take their chances in the dark, cold water of the bay…and Marion Boyle couldn't swim.

Without receiving orders, not sparing a second thought—even without stopping to get one of the fort's boats—the seven soldiers on shore dove into the water and started swimming toward the fire. Privates Robert Murie and David A. Wagner weren't up to the distance or the strong current and had to go back, but Privates William Sharp, Henry Ackers and Walter K. Wilbraham struggled through the half-mile swim and reached the scene. Wilbraham valiantly boarded the cruiser, practically in the midst of the flames. Booth informed Wilbraham that the fire had been caused by an explosion ignited by a leak in one of the engine's gasoline pipes and that a second explosion might well be imminent. Immediately, Wilbraham focused his efforts on Marion Boyle, helping her into a life preserver and then into the water, where Ackers and Sharp were waiting. While these two soldiers worked together to support Boyle above the water throughout the long, exhausting swim back to Fort Adams, Wilbraham stayed on the burning vessel to help Booth try to

Fort Adams

Fort Adams service club. This was a place of relaxation and entertainment for off-duty soldiers. *National Archives/Daniel P. Titus Collection.*

extinguish the fire and was soon joined by Privates Thomas Sheridan and Robert Fitz-Henry.

Meanwhile, the fire had also been spotted by men at the fort's officers' club, as well as some soldiers at Fort Wetherill, and boats were quickly launched from both bases. The four men gratefully boarded the Fort Adams boats while Fort Wetherill's motor mine yawls took over the firefighting. When the blaze was finally quenched, the M-boats towed the embattled cruiser to Fort Adams.

Lieutenant Booth and Marion Boyle were both taken to Fort Adams's infirmary as soon as they arrived on shore. Both were suffering from shock, exposure and burns on their hands and faces from their attempts to try to put out the fire themselves before help arrived. Even so, Miss Boyle's injuries were not serious enough to warrant an overnight stay: a fort ambulance took her back to her own home later that same night. The five soldiers who came to their aid suffered no injuries.

It wasn't long before commendations started rolling in for the seven men whose bravery had made headlines. Even Murie and Wagner, who began the rescue attempt but could not complete it, were included when, on July 24, Brigadier General Ralph E. Haines, commander of all Narragansett Bay defenses, officially cited all seven men for their "heroic action in overcoming difficulties of the swift current and cold water of the channel," their willingness to aid others with a "disregard of personal danger" and their "presence of mind" and "quick judgment," all of which had "averted a tragedy" and "reflects great credit upon the entire command."[73] Very likely as a direct result of this honor, twenty-two-year-old Wilbraham was promoted to the rank of corporal the following September.

Exactly six months to the day after his participation in the dramatic rescue at sea, on January 14, 1942, Corporal Wilbraham was driving along snow-covered Ruggles Avenue in Newport, along with two fellow soldiers. Private First Class George J. Puskar rode beside Wilbraham, while Private Joseph W. Brown occupied the back seat. It was still early in the evening, 6:20 p.m., but the truncated daylight of winter had already given way to darkness. Wilbraham lost control of the vehicle. The car skidded on the slippery surface, slewed off the road and spun for fifteen feet before crashing into a tree.

All three men were rushed to the Fort Adams hospital as soon as an ambulance could reach them. Brown escaped with only a broken jaw and some other minor injuries, but Puskar and Wilbraham both suffered fractured skulls. Puskar died that night; Wilbraham fought for his life for two days, but he followed Puskar in death at 12:17 a.m. on the morning of January 17. Having kept tragic death from others, he was powerless to prevent his own.

On June 11, 1942, five months after Wilbraham's untimely death, the *Newport Daily News* reported that Wilbraham and his six companions in the rescue of Lieutenant Booth and Marion Boyle were awarded the Soldier's Medal, the highest honor given for valor outside of combat. Wilbraham's medal was accepted by his widow.

As the war progressed, it became evident that there was little need for coastal defenses to exist at all, since neither German nor Japanese forces had the power to mount a significant assault on the American mainland. As a result, coastal fortifications were gradually reduced, with many personnel being reclassified for combat duty overseas. By the end of the war in Europe in May 1945, the bay's harbor defenses consisted of only four companies—this was down from a peak strength of eighteen companies in two regiments that had functioned in the area in late 1940.

But the end of the war did not mean the end of the U-boat threat. At 5:40 p.m. on May 5, 1945, German sub *U-853* attacked and sank

Cook with a coal-fired range in a kitchen in the south wall casemates. *John S. and Margaret D. Dugan Collection.*

Above: Soldiers march in formation during a review in about the 1930s. *John S. and Margaret D. Dugan Collection.*

Opposite, top: Army trucks that may be taking the soldiers to Sachuest Point in Middletown for rifle practice. Note the observation post on top of the fort. *John S. and Margaret D. Dugan Collection.*

Opposite, bottom: Soldiers and an officer line up for chow at a mobile kitchen range in about the 1930s. *John S. and Margaret D. Dugan Collection.*

an American merchant collier called the *Black Point* off the coast of Point Judith in southern Rhode Island, despite having received orders from Admiral Dönitz commanding all vessels to return to Germany in anticipation of an imminent surrender to the Allies. The next day, the naval destroyer escort USS *Atherton* (DE-169) and patrol frigate USS *Moberly* (PF-63) engaged and sank the German vessel with a series of depth charges, resulting in the loss of all hands—fifty-five men—on the sub.

FORT ADAMS

WACs, WORKERS AND WIVES:
WOMEN IN THE LIFE OF FORT ADAMS

I desire you would Remember the Ladies.
—*Abigail Adams, 1776*[74]

A running joke among the Fort Adams staff is that male visitors bribe their wives into a fort tour in exchange for allowing the ladies to drag them along on shopping excursions in downtown Newport later in the day. There is a kernel of truth in the joke, but the perception that Fort Adams is a "guy place" is unfortunate—not to mention inaccurate. From its very beginnings, women have played vital roles in the life of Fort Adams. Their presence throughout the years is testified by a total of thirty-three graves in the post cemetery engraved with women's names.[75]

Although women had surely been present as officers' wives and other family members since the fort was first garrisoned in 1841, the earliest specific reference we can find to women taking an active part in handling a crisis within the community comes in January 1909, when the *Newport Daily News* and *Newport Mercury* reported that Corporal Nelson Henry had attempted to kill his wife, Ellen, only three days earlier, by shooting her three times before ending his own life. As their mother struggled for her life, all three of the Henry family's little ones entered the care of family friends who also lived at the fort. Ellen was not expected to live. Although the fort's physicians were making every effort their skill and the era's medical technology allowed, they held little hope and believed that her wounds would in the end prove fatal. There was every indication that her little children would soon be completely orphaned.

Miraculously, however, on January 2 (the day of the corporal's funeral), the *Newport Daily News* reported that Ellen Henry was recovering against all odds. Four days after the shooting, Ellen was expected to make a full recovery, displaying the remarkable strength of a mother who will trample down death itself for the sake of her children. In its January 4 edition, the *Daily News* observed that the recovering Mrs. Henry was being assisted and cared for by "the women of the garrison."[76] Although these ladies surely had more than enough to occupy them, tending to their own households and families, they went out of their way—without being asked—to help their neighbor in dire need.

WAACS AT FORT ADAMS ARE SWORN INTO THE ARMY AS WACS

Women taking the oath to enter the Women's Army Corps in August 1943. Fort Adams's chapel is behind and to the left of the group. *John T. Hopf*/Newport Daily News.

Unfortunately, records of women's presence at Fort Adams become scarce after this for the next several decades, but during the time of the Second World War, women once again appear at the forefront of the Fort Adams community. During this time, women began to branch out from domestic roles into positions of employment, both as civilians and as members of the United States Army. A priceless photograph that appeared in the *Newport Daily News* on August 11, 1943, shows members of the Women's Army Auxiliary Corps (WAAC) being sworn in as members of the newly formed Women's Army Corps (WAC). Their commanding officer, Lieutenant Martha McQuaid, stands nearby while Fort Adams's adjutant, Lieutenant Colonel George A. Bates, administers the oath.[77] These "WACs" chiefly served in the fort's offices as clerks, telephone operators and communications workers.

In a 2003 interview for the Fort Adams Oral History Project, Constance A. Casey recalled that two WACs worked with her in the Artillery Engineers office. Mrs. Casey began there as a civilian worker in November 1941—just one month before the attack on Pearl Harbor.[78] The day after the attack, as she drove through the entrance on her way to work, she noted the increased security measures: guards had established

View of southeast and southwest walls in the early twentieth century. *John S. and Margaret D. Dugan Collection.*

checkpoints at all entrances and later began searching trunks of cars. Civilian workers did not live on fort property but rather drove in each day or took the bus from their homes.

Mrs. Casey remembered Fort Adams fondly, describing its atmosphere as being "a very relaxed place to work...like a big happy family...it was a lovely place to work. Everybody was so friendly and nice and got along so well together." In the artillery office, her duties consisted of filing and other general office work, some of which sounds like medieval torture in the computer era. Constance took dictation in shorthand on a lined pad and transcribed the notes on a manual Royal typewriter, making two copies of each document on carbon paper.

During her ten years as a civilian professional at Fort Adams, Constance transferred to the dispensary in the post hospital when the artillery office was closed and then again to the transportation office. Each new position brought new challenges as Constance had to learn terms and procedures specific to each office. Working with the ship-

to-shore radio was one of the more fun parts of her job. She even remembered hearing her boss communicating with naval personnel about plans for the anti-submarine net to be installed in the East Passage (see the section on the Second World War). But some of her fondest memories were of the social events at the fort. Constance recalled that the Fort Adams dances were mostly formal, evening-dress affairs, but at times, there would be occasions for "wacky, fun clothes" along the lines of costume parties. Mrs. Casey also remembered the "quadrangle"—the mid-twentieth-century designation for the parade field within the stone fort—as quarters for the military personnel and their families. She didn't go there often, as there was no need for civilian workers to visit that part of the fort in the course of their workday.

Doris V. Shoesmith, another participant in the Oral History Project, was one of the denizens of those old officers' quarters.[79] Doris's husband, electrician Harold Shoesmith, was stationed at Fort Adams from 1941 to 1944 as a tech sergeant. Doris was only twenty-two years old and newly married, and this military posting was her first time away from home. The couple had lived in Middletown until the declaration of war, whereupon Harold was immediately given quarters at the fort. The things that most stood out for Doris about these quarters "in the wall" were the large size of the rooms, the distinctive pocket doors, the high ceilings and a black stove in the kitchen. Old rifle loopholes had been altered to serve as "windows," but these had not been screened; Mrs. Shoesmith's reminiscences suggest that there was no way to close them, at least not completely. Snow and wind would blow in, but because of the narrowness of the loopholes on the outside and the great thickness of the wall, these wintery elements couldn't get a real foothold in the home beyond the window frames that had been fitted to the inside of the loopholes and embrasures.

After moving in, Harold was assigned to the searchlight batteries and, as a result, was on night duty most of the time. Mrs. Shoesmith became the mother of two children during her time at Fort Adams and spent the vast majority of her time, as had so many of her predecessors in the fort's history, caring for them and running the household. As a busy homemaker, one of the only entertainments she was able to pursue was attending the shows at Fort Adams's small movie theater.

There must not have been much time for leisure—the pressures on Fort Adams housewives was far greater than in civilian households. "We had inspections, so you had to keep things up," Doris recalled. "You never knew when they were going to come in. You had to keep your quarters up, that's for sure…You couldn't have anything broken. I painted, I varnished everything to be ready when they came in. My father put a brand-new floor in that house where we lived in the wall." On one occasion, to Sergeant Shoesmith's great chagrin, the Shoesmith children painted a wall of the family quarters with silver radiator paint just before an inspection—perhaps trying to do their part to spruce the place up!

Doris remembered that although the fort's own commissary and Post Exchange (the "PX") had a good selection, it was sometimes necessary to travel by bus into town or have goods delivered when she wanted some special item not available in the fort's stores. Fort Adams was quite insular, a self-contained and self-sufficient community—more like a small town than a military base. She described her life there as "uneventful" but "peaceful. Life was quiet here."

Where there are mothers, there are, of course, children. Fort Adams was home to countless children of all ages during its 150 active years. Siblings

A family at Fort Adams around the time of the First World War. *Fort Adams Trust.*

Barbara Hamill-Platt and Roy Hamill recalled the fort in the 1930s and early 1940s, when their father was stationed as a first sergeant in Company F, Thirteenth Infantry. Likewise, Madeleine Rondeau remembered living at Fort Adams as a young child with her family, including her younger brother and sister, when her father, Master Sergeant Ephraim Mandeville, served in charge of the fort's boathouse and NCO club.[80]

Like all children, the youth of Fort Adams found all manner of mischief to get into, chiefly consisting of exploring the tunnels and climbing atop the (very dangerous) ramparts. During this time, Fort Adams families referred to the parade field as the "quadrangle"—a common term for such an area but in this case a misnomer, as the field is enclosed by five sides rather than four. Nevertheless, when former residents state that their families were assigned quarters in "the quadrangle," they mean the former officers' quarters surrounding the six-and-a-half-acre parade field. Especially during the time of World War II, the "quad" became a playground for the many children living at the fort. Mule rides also provided an exciting diversion from time to time.

Fort Adams

Above: Mule barn and mules in the late 1800s. *National Archives/Daniel P. Titus.*

Opposite, top: Children of the Hamill family at Fort Adams in the 1930s. *Fort Adams Trust.*

Opposite, bottom: Children inside Fort Adams near the east gate, perhaps awaiting the bus to take them to school in Newport. *John S. and Margaret D. Dugan Collection.*

Both the Hamill siblings and Mrs. Rondeau recalled Fort Adams during the terrible Hurricane of 1938, which remains one of the strongest and deadliest storms on record for the New England region. While power in parts of the fort was lost for a time, the great granite walls withstood the force of the tempest with no damage. In fact, the hurricane was responsible for Madeleine Rondeau's family being assigned quarters in the fort—while her father had already been stationed there, the family lived on Thames Street until the hurricane flooded their home, resulting in the army giving them quarters on base.

Mrs. Rondeau also recalled an incident rather frightening to contemplate: she remembered her father swearing that a German submarine had come after one of the mine planters on which he was working in the East Passage of Narragansett Bay before the submarine nets were lowered and the U-boat's entry was prevented. "Once in a while," Madeleine remembered, her father "would take us into Newport in a PT boat, and we thought that was really something."

Irene Gilles at the organ in Fort Adams's chapel, with the soldiers' choir. *Fort Adams Trust.*

Chapel at Fort Adams decorated with flowers—possibly for a wedding. *Fort Adams Trust.*

Schoolmates of Fort Adams children also thought it was "really something" to see their friends arrive at school in an army truck. Generally, the local school bus would drive right into the parade field to pick up students who resided at Fort Adams, but on days when the bus broke down, military vehicles would make sure that the children got to school on time.

Newport native Irene (Rena) Murphy Gilles was also a civilian but had a different kind of job at the fort: volunteer organist for the soldiers' choir who provided the music for the Sunday morning Roman Catholic Masses held in the Fort Adams chapel.[81] Ms. Gilles wrote a brief memoir of her time at Fort Adams, and to honor that effort, we present her story in her own words:[82]

> *My experience with Fort Adams began in the summer of 1943 when my piano teacher, Josephine McHenry, asked if I would be willing to try my hand at accompanying a soldier choir at the fort. I had never played an organ and could not use the pedals, but this was a Hammond electric organ and close enough to a piano to get the job done. The choir consisted of ten men soldiers, directed by Jim Dalton, and holding practise [sic] sessions every Thursday evening. A driver named Romeo Messier from Fall River, MA would pick me up at my home…in an army staff car and drive me to and from practise. Romeo drove like the wind through the dark streets; blackout was in effect and there were no street lights. It was at once exciting and terrifying but we always managed to arrive in one piece.*
>
> *The practise was held in the non-denominational Chapel…The Catholic Chaplain was Father James Cloonan who hailed from Tipperary, Ireland and was probably on loan from the diocese of Florida. He was a charmer, a man's man, and well suited to his role. He loved his work, his driver, Romeo, and hamburgers from the R.I. Lunch which he affectionately referred to as "the greasy spoon." The choir director had sung in and had some experience with choirs and the results were very good with our group. The soloist was Bernie White, a teacher from Webster, MA, who had a nice singing voice. The men were all attached to the 10th Coastal Artillery Battalion and, for the most part, were older than regular draftees and not classified as IA due to either age or vision limitations. They were a great bunch and more than kind to this sixteen year old. After rehearsal we used to walk to the recreation center where there was music for dancing. Local girls would be brought to the Center by bus for a couple of hours.*

A family sitting on the parade ground of Fort Adams. The east gate is to the left. *Fort Adams Trust.*

Maude Allen was the hostess at the Fort Recreation Center and she ran a pretty tight ship, making sure everyone was on their best behavior. On Sunday mornings she always had a big pot of coffee ready after Mass and some kind of pastry or muffins to go with it. I had my first cup of coffee there, using evaporated milk and no sugar. Tasted awful but I would never have admitted as much.

Occasionally Father Cloonan would have to say two other Masses, one at Fort Church in Tiverton, and one at Fort Wetherill in Jamestown. I only went to Tiverton once and have no idea where the camp there was located. Someone had rounded up a barrel organ that had to be hand pumped to force air through the bellows. It was less than heavenly music, more like the sound of someone having an asthma attack.

The whole unit was transferred sometime in 1944 and went to Camp Forest, TN. Father Cloonan was sent to a camp in Georgia…After the war, Father Cloonan returned to Florida and was pastor of a very large parish in Jacksonville where I visited him once in the late 50s…

Maude Allen retired in Newport and lived on Coggeshall Ave in a big stone house, probably on the corner of Ruggles.

Fort Adams will always have a special place in my heart. The whole experience left me with wonderful memories which I treasure to this day.

PART IV
FALL AND RISE

Twilight Years

After the Second World War, Fort Adams, along with all other coast defense fortifications, found itself a vestige of a bygone era. In this brief interlude between the periods of coast defense guns and antiaircraft missiles, the concept of coastal defense revolved around antiaircraft guns. While Fort Adams remained the headquarters post for the entirety of Narragansett Bay Harbor Defenses (NBHD), with Forts Church and Greene as subposts, it became clear that Fort Adams, along with all other coast defense installations, was no longer needed by the army.

In November 1945, Rhode Island governor John O. Pastore, along with a group of citizens led by philanthropist John Nicholas Brown, decided to offer Fort Adams to the United Nations Organization as a site for its permanent home. The UN declined the offer, making its headquarters instead in New York City and allowing Fort Adams to continue as a military installation. However, its garrison was reduced to the point that disabled veterans from both world wars were employed as gate guards.

At 3:40 a.m. on Sunday, April 13, 1947, a sailor standing watch on the destroyer tender USS *Yosemite* caught sight of flames in the upstairs barracks on the southeast wall of the old fort. Fortunately, the barracks

Soldiers on parade on Thames Street in downtown Newport. This was probably a Fourth of July parade. *Fort Adams Trust.*

were unoccupied at the time. The *Yosemite* radioed Newport's Naval Training Station, which in turn notified Fort Adams by telephone. The fort's units, composing the 250-man garrison stationed at the fort, were aided by the Naval Training Station, as well as the city's fire department, in subduing the blaze. Although the fire was successfully extinguished, the southeast barracks were reduced to a burnt shell, never to be rebuilt. It was an eerie symbol that Fort Adams's best days were over. The beginning of the fort's last days was marked by the retirement of one of its final commanding officers, Colonel Metzger, whose successor, Colonel Edward B. McCarthy, would oversee initial preparations for Fort Adams's final deactivation. These were taken over and continued by the fort's last commander, Major B.H. Schimmel.

Fort Adams was finally closed as a coast defense installation in June 1950—the same month as the outbreak of the Korean War. The fact that an army post was deactivated at the beginning of a war indicated the obsolescence of coastal artillery. Only the small 1112th Area Service

Bunks in upstairs barracks. *National Archives/Daniel P. Titus Collection.*

Unit (ASU), also known as the "Narragansett Bay Marine Repair Shop," remained at Fort Adams to maintain military boats and other equipment involved in antiaircraft training in the Narragansett Bay area. Even this unit departed on June 30, 1952. From then on, Fort Adams, once the proudest glory of the greatest military power the world had ever seen, was a desolate shell, its usefulness outlived, left to fall into ruins.

In 1953, the United States Army turned Fort Adams over to the navy, which used the old structure as a storage facility and utilized the plush homes of Officers' Row to the south of the main fort as housing for senior naval officers stationed at the Naval War College, located in Newport on Coaster's Harbor Island. In the late 1950s, the navy built additional officers' quarters near the fort, which to this day remain in use by War College officers and their families.

On August 23, 1956, Rear Admiral Ralph Earle Jr., commanding officer of the naval base at Newport, wrote to the Newport Historical Society to inform it that the navy was planning to tear Fort Adams down. In this communication, the commander remarked that the fort, though an old structure and "a familiar landmark," was also "without major historical associations or significance" and for that reason "is an unlikely candidate for national shrine or park status. It has long outlived its usefulness…is in an advanced state of deterioration…and is beyond economical repair. It is difficult to police, dangerous to children of Naval personnel presently housed on the reservation, a possible source of nuisance and vandalism, and a definite fire and safety hazard."[83]

The rear admiral certainly had good points in referring to the physical dangers to life and limb that the fort had begun to pose. He was also correct in noting that the federal government simply did not have the funding available to do the work required to make the fort structurally sound. At the same time, the irony of the letter cannot be overlooked: while it is true that no major battle ever occurred at Fort Adams, a good argument can be made that invasion and combat do not provide the sole criteria for historical value. Besides, the site certainly had seen action during the Revolution, when the guns where Fort Adams would later stand drove off the British Royal Navy several times, delaying the occupation of Newport and buying the time needed for Rhode Island to officially declare itself separated from the British Parliament. Additionally, the fort had historical associations with the navy itself, having partnered with that service branch as host of the Naval Academy (albeit briefly) in 1861.

The commander's letter succinctly outlined the navy's plan "to dismantle the structure and to salvage the granite blocks," which would "be incorporated into a 2,500-foot breakwater planned for the Coddington Cove area to create an inner harbor for the protection of ships at the existing pier and at a second pier soon to be under construction."[84] As for the memory of Fort Adams? At the far end of the breakwater, near a beacon tower, "a suitably inscribed plaque" would be placed to inform the public "as to the source of the granite."[85] In concluding the letter, Rear Admiral Earle invited the historical society's response.

The whole city of Newport took him up on the invitation. A plaque atop the rubble of their former home, of which they had been proud and where fond memories had taken root, would have no doubt appeared as Fort Adams's gravestone to the local citizens still living in Newport who had lived and worked there, especially during the Second World War (only eleven years distant in 1956). The public outcry against the navy's plan was deafening. Vocal protest saved the fort from destruction, and as a result of the associated publicity, wider public interest in rehabilitating the fort was ignited. Another decade would pass, though, before decisive action was taken.

From September 4 to 10, 1958, and again from August 29 to September 23, 1960, "Quarters One" at Fort Adams, built to serve as the home of the fort's commanding officer in 1873, served in a

Commanding officers' quarters, completed in 1876. *Fort Adams Trust.*

new capacity—as the "summer White House" to President Dwight D. Eisenhower while he vacationed in Newport.[86] This earned Quarters One the nickname "the Eisenhower House," by which the elegant building is still known today.[87]

Looking to offload the white elephant that was Fort Adams, the navy in 1965 turned over the fort complex as well as the adjacent waterfront property to the State of Rhode Island for use as a state park, clearing the way for efforts to restore Fort Adams with the goal of eventually opening it to the public. These efforts were led by Senator Erich A. O'D. Taylor, Senator Claiborne Pell, Antoinette Downing of the Rhode Island Historic Preservation Commission and John Nicholas Brown (who had previously been involved in the effort to get the UN headquartered at the fort), among many others. This cadre of influential individuals—concerned for the preservation of history and the part Fort Adams played not only in defense of the nation but also in a more intimate capacity as a bastion of the community—formed the basis for the State of Rhode Island to establish the Fort Adams Foundation in 1976. The purpose of this organization was to redevelop and preserve the fort, laying the groundwork for all future restoration efforts.

FALL AND RISE

RESTORATION: FROM 1965 TO THE EARLY TWENTY-FIRST CENTURY

In 1972, the Fort Adams Foundation appointed Mr. George Howarth as the fort's "commandant," tasked with overseeing daily operations that—it was hoped—would result in redeveloping the fort for the benefit of the general public. With this goal in mind, the fort was opened for tours on September 4, 1972—the first time the fort had been accessed in twenty years. It was a sign of the great interest in Fort Adams that about two thousand people took advantage of the opportunity. Thus began the use of Fort Adams as a major tourist attraction and event center until 1980.

During this time, the world-renowned Newport Jazz Festival began holding its annual summertime concerts at Fort Adams.[88] Over the years, many notable performers have graced the stages of both the Jazz and Folk Festivals, including jazz legends Ella Fitzgerald, Billie Holiday and

A 24-pounder casemate cannon mounted on an authentically re-created casemate carriage. The cannon may be original to Fort Adams. *Kathleen Troost-Cramer.*

Loophole window in jail cell. *Kathleen Troost-Cramer.*

Carmen McRae; folk greats Peter, Paul and Mary; and even the Boston Pops Esplanade Orchestra, conducted by Arthur Fiedler.

The efforts of the Fort Adams Foundation resulted in the fort's being declared a National Historic Landmark by the secretary of the interior in 1977. This is the highest distinction a structure can possess relating to its architectural and historical significance, and the honor is rather rare: only 2,300 structures in the United States bear this designation.

Fort Adams gained a bit of star credential when the PBS film adaptation of Nathaniel Hawthorne's classic novel *The Scarlet Letter* was filmed in part of the fort's former officers' quarters in 1978. In that same year (unrelated to the filming), the vintage navy housing on the fort's property, abandoned since 1973, was either torn down or relocated to different parts of Aquidneck Island in order to make more open land available for use as recreational space.

Just two years later, efforts to revive the fort suffered a major setback with the death of Senator Erich Taylor, Fort Adams's biggest supporter in the Rhode Island state legislature. Many other factors—such as budget shortfalls, safety concerns and the reassignment of the fort's overseer Howarth—led to the fort's being closed to the public, left to the merciless march of time, the brutal seashore elements and vandalism for the next thirteen years.

Then, in 1993, hope surfaced once again when the Army Corps of Engineers announced that it planned to embark upon a $500,000 endeavor to restore Fort Adams for public access. This led to renewed interest in the fort, and the Fort Adams Foundation was revitalized under the leadership of Mr. Edwin Connelly of Jamestown, Colonel Frank Hale of the Newport Artillery Company and Senator Teresa Paiva-Weed of Newport, who had served as a guide when the fort had been opened for tours briefly in the late 1970s.

The Army Corps of Engineers' project was finally realized in the summer of 1995. Work included the removal of debris from the casemates, placing safety railings in hazardous areas and planting a "fence" of shrubbery to limit access to the west wall, which had been damaged by at least two fires in the 1960s to the point of becoming structurally unsound. These efforts were complemented by a state initiative to install handicap-accessible ramps. The end result was that Fort Adams could safely host visitors once again. The gates opened in May 1995 for both regular tours and public events. The fort's potential as a major event center was demonstrated on May 18, 1997, when an estimated crowd of eight thousand turned out for the first Fort Adams Adventure Day. In that same year, the National Park Service added to Fort Adams's designations by declaring it to be a Landmark at Risk.

Above: The restored casemates at the north end of Fort Adams's parade ground. *Kathleen Troost-Cramer.*

Opposite, top: Exterior of jail cells in the restored redoubt/jail outside the east gate. *Kathleen Troost-Cramer.*

Opposite, bottom: The overnight barracks, formerly the officers' quarters. *Kathleen Troost-Cramer.*

On July 4, 1999, Fort Adams celebrated its 200th anniversary with an open house attended by Senator Claiborne Pell and Congressman Patrick Kennedy as special guests and U.S. Senator Jack Reed as keynote speaker. A twenty-one-gun salute was fired jointly by the Rhode Island National Guard and members of the Newport Artillery Company— the same militia that had fired from the very same spot more than two centuries before, driving British vessels of war into retreat in pursuit of American sovereignty.

In October 1999, Colonel Anthony Palermo, USMC (Ret.), was hired as the executive director of the Fort Adams Trust, a private nonprofit that had been established in 1994 to take over the tasks of the Fort Adams Foundation in managing the restoration, preservation and educational

Fort Adams

FALL AND RISE

Above: Colonel Robert Edenbach and the Newport Artillery Company fire a Model 1841 6-pounder gun during a Civil War reenactment at Fort Adams. *Fort Adams Trust.*

Opposite, top: One of the bunkrooms of the overnight barracks. *Kathleen Troost-Cramer.*

Opposite, bottom: The "mess hall" of the overnight barracks. *Kathleen Troost-Cramer.*

efforts at the fort. In the spring of the following year, Mary Beth Smith was hired as the trust's director of operations, and around the same time, on May 13, Fort Adams was rededicated as a National Historic Landmark. Colonel Frank Hale, RIM, was also proclaimed Honorary Commandant of Fort Adams by Governor Lincoln Almond. The day was celebrated with the help of a large display of historic military vehicles and a number of uniformed reenactors representing the manifold periods in which the fort had stood guard over one of the nation's most strategic natural resources, Newport Harbor and Narragansett Bay.

The real sign that Fort Adams had revived, though, was the raising of the new flag in April 2001, with a ninety-foot flagpole erected in the northeast corner close to the original location of the fort's garrison flag. The occasion was a nostalgic one, since the colors had not flown over Fort Adams for the past fifty years. This event, attended by the Rhode Island National Guard and Newport Artillery Company as color guard, marked the official beginning of

Restored interior of the north wall casemates. Note the outstanding condition of the brickwork, more than a century and a half after construction. *Kathleen Troost-Cramer.*

the Fort Adams Trust's restoration program. Funded by a grant of $350,000 from the State of Rhode Island, this early effort also included stabilization of the northeast bastion, the placement of instructional signs throughout the fort and the installation of safety features to prevent access to danger areas and preserve select locations for future work.

Today, visitors can see for themselves the breathtaking progress the trust has made toward restoring and stabilizing the fort in an effort to make more parts of the fort accessible to the public. Much of this work is not visible as it involved stabilization of the roofs and interior structures, but the restoration of the north casemates (completed in 2003), quartermaster's area and the lower portions of the west wall are obvious at even a cursory glance. Period-accurate lampposts were installed around the parade field in 2006, and an overnight barracks, restored in the same year, now occupies a section of the former officers' quarters in the east wall, with modern amenities for overnight stays by groups desiring such an experience at the fort. In a welcome revival of

Fort Adams's historical relationship with the United States Navy, the restored northeast casemates host a display from the Naval War College Museum focusing on Narragansett Bay defenses from the Revolution to World War II, as well as Newport's history-altering trade with Japan.

In 2008, the old redoubt, built in 1842 and converted to the fort stockade in 1867, was fully restored, and at the time of this writing, it serves as the Fort Adams gift shop and trust offices. Visitors can view the old jail cells, where a soldier was once held on suspicion of murdering his friend.[89] Thanks to the open spaces referendum on the 2010 ballot, as well as a grant from Preserve America's Treasures, the fort was back in shape enough to allow self-guided tours of the parade field area.

One might say that Fort Adams is only now beginning to wage battle, for the first time in its history—and for its very survival. Restoration efforts struggle day by day to keep ahead of the elements, to hold at bay the destructive forces of wind and salt spray and not merely stop the crumbling grip of time but actually turn back the clock to show the glory this great structure once possessed, to people it once again by preserving its stories. Long may Fort Adams stand guard. In showing us our past, it teaches us our future.

APPENDIX A
COMMANDING OFFICERS
OF FORT ADAMS

This listing is the result of many hours of painstaking work. The authors have endeavored to be as accurate and complete as possible.

The primary references employed in creating this list are Cullum's *Register of Graduates of the United States Military Academy*, Heitman's *Historical Dictionary and Register of the United States Army*, local newspapers, Newport city directories and the *Newport Social Index*. Cullum's register provides a detailed synopsis of the careers of every West Point graduate from its founding in 1802 through 1920. As most of Fort Adams's commanders were West Point graduates, this is an outstanding resource. (A copy, in seven volumes, is available in Newport's Redwood Library.) Heitman's register contains a listing of every regular army officer from 1784 through 1903, including regimental assignment and dates of promotion.

Common military abbreviations have been used. After each officer's name is the date of his entry into the army as an officer. "Non-MA" indicates that the officer is not a graduate of the United States Military Academy at West Point. Officers without the "Non-MA" qualifier are West Point graduates. Ordinal numbers (i.e., 1st, 2nd and so on) indicate the number of the regiment to which the officer belonged. All officers are members of artillery regiments unless indicated otherwise.

The information is listed in the following order: the officer's rank, the officer's name, the year of his graduation from West Point (in cases

Appendix A

of non–West Point graduates, the first year of commissioned service), regimental or corps assignment (AC: Artillery Corps; CAC: Coast Artillery Corps) and regiment of assignment. All officers are assumed to be of the artillery unless otherwise indicated.

Note on Brevet Ranks

Anyone making a study of the U.S. Army of the nineteenth century will often encounter officers with brevet ranks. Prior to the Spanish-American War, it was common for officers to be rewarded for exemplary service with brevet appointments. A brevet entitled an officer to wear the uniform and receive the courtesies of a higher rank but not the pay and command authority. In cases where a commander held a brevet commission, his regular army rank is listed first and his brevet rank in parentheses. Officers were usually referred to by their brevet ranks, as was the case with Brevet Major General George Custer, who held a regular army commission as a lieutenant colonel when he was killed in 1876. In cases where an officer was promoted during his tenure as commanding officer, the higher rank is indicated.

"Old" Fort Adams (1799–1824)

Note: Old Fort Adams was a subpost of Fort Wolcott throughout its history.

CPT John Henry, Non-MA '98, 2nd Arts and Engs, July 4, 1799–as of July 21, 1800
Unknown, July 22–October 27, 1800
LT John Knight, Non-MA '98, 2nd Arts and Engs, as of October 28, 1800–probably January 1801
CPT William Steele, Non-MA '97, 2nd Arts and Engs, January 1801–October 7, 1801
Unknown, October 7, 1801–March 31, 1802

Appendix A

Note: On April 1, 1802, the company assigned to Fort Adams was consolidated with Captain Beall's company stationed at Fort Wolcott. There is no evidence that Fort Adams was garrisoned from that date until the War of 1812.

MAJ John Wood, Non-MA '08, RI Militia, July 25, 1814–February 23, 1815 (commanded two hundred Rhode Island militiamen of a unit called Wood's State Corps, which was organized into three companies, assigned to Fort Adams; Major Wood previously served as the first lieutenant of the Artillery Company of Newport)
CPT Armstrong Irvine, '11, Lt Art, possibly May 17, 1815–circa 1816
CPT John S. Peyton, Non-MA '12, Lt Art, furloughed on October 20, 1815 (resigned on April 1, 1816)
1LT William Hobart, Non-MA, Lt Art, as of February 29, 1816–as of May 31, 1816
CPT John L. Eastman, Non-MA '08, Lt Art (Co. G), as of March 1816– as of November 30, 1819 (in command of both Fort Adams and Fort Wolcott)
CPT John H. Wilkins (Co. D), as of January 31, 1820–as of April 30, 1820
CPT Henry Knox Craig, Non-MA '12, Lt Art (Co. I), as of May 31, 1820–as of April 30, 1821 (transferred to 3rd Artillery on June 1, 1821; he was chief of ordnance from 1851 to 1861, retired in 1863 and was brevetted to brigadier general in 1865)

Note: Old Fort Adams was probably deactivated on June 1, 1821, when the army was reorganized with fewer artillery units.

Construction of New Fort Adams (1824–1857)

The officers listed here were the senior engineers in Newport and were in charge of construction at the fort. Construction was not continuous.

1LT Andrew Talcott, '18, CE, August 10, 1824–February 21, 1825
LTC Joseph G. Totten, '05, CE, February 22, 1825–December 7, 1838 (appointed chief engineer of the army with rank of colonel on December 8, 1838)

APPENDIX A

1LT James L. Mason, '36, CE, December 8, 1838–1845
1LT Henry L. Eustis, '42, CE, circa 1845–November 30, 1849 (resigned)
1LT William Stark Rosecrans, '42, CE, December 1, 1849–circa 1853 (remained in Newport until April 1, 1854; rose to major general during the Civil War; was engineer for the construction of St. Mary's Church in Newport from 1849 to 1853)
CPT George Dutton, '22, CE, circa 1853–circa 1856
1LT Edward B. Hunt, '45, CE, April 5, 1855–October 17, 1857 (killed in New York in 1863 while developing an experimental weapon system)

"NEW" FORT ADAMS (1841–1952) AND PRE–CIVIL WAR (1841–1861)

MAJ Matthew M. Payne, Non-MA '12, 2nd, August 25, 1841–July 2, 1842
LTC Alexander C.W. Fanning, '12, 2nd, July 3, 1842–as of July 1, 1843
CPT Francis Taylor, '25, 1st (interim), August 29, 1843–September 12, 1843
LTC Benjamin K. Pierce, Non-MA '12, 1st, September 13, 1843–August 18, 1845 (brother of future president Franklin Pierce)
CPT Francis Taylor, '25, 1st (interim), August 19, 1845–September 14, 1845
CPT Henry Swartwout, '32, 2nd, September 15, 1845–May 30, 1846
CPT Charles S. Merchant, '14, 2nd, May 31, 1846–September 30, 1846

Note: Fort Adams was left with a caretaking detachment of one corporal and three privates. Also note that during the Mexican-American War (1847–48), the highest-ranking officer at the fort is listed.

CPT Joseph S. Pitman, Non-MA '47, 9th Inf., March 11, 1847–March 26, 1847
Unknown, March 27–April 2, 1847
CPT Lorenzo Johnson, Non-MA '47, 9th Inf., April 3, 1847–April 25, 1847
COL Truman B. Ransom, Non-MA '47, 9th Inf., April 26, 1847–May 18, 1847 (Colonel Ransom was killed leading his men in battle during the Battle of Chapultepec in Mexico)

Appendix A

BG Franklin Pierce, Non-MA '47, May 19–May 28, 1847 (Pierce departed from Fort Adams for Mexico with the last contingent of the 9th Infantry Regiment; he served as president of the United States from 1853 to 1857)
Unknown, May 29–July 5, 1848 (probably left in caretaking status)
LTC Benjamin K. Pierce, Non-MA '12, 1st, as of July 31, 1847–September 26, 1848 (brother of future president Franklin Pierce; in command of a small caretaking detachment; died on April 1, 1850)
CPT (B/MAJ) Francis O. Wyse, '37, 3rd, September 27, 1848–September 30, 1848
COL William Gates, '06, 3rd, October 1, 1848–July 31, 1853
CPT Henry B. Judd, '39, 3rd, August 1, 1853–September 23, 1853
1LT Sewall L. Fremont, '41, 3rd, September 24, 1853–October 19, 1853

Note: Fort Adams was in caretaker status from October 20, 1853, to May 28, 1857.

1LT Asher R. Eddy, '44, 1st, May 29, 1857–June 12, 1857
CPT (Brevet LTC) John Bankhead Magruder, '30, 1st, June 13, 1857–October 31, 1859 (major general in the Confederate States Army during the Civil War)
Ordnance Sergeant Mark W. Smith, November 1, 1859–April 18, 1861 (Ordnance Sergeant Smith enlisted in the army in 1827, was a veteran of the Mexican-American War and was wounded in the Battle of Chapultepec; he arrived at Fort Adams in September 1859, and in 1863, he was transferred to Fort Griswold in Groton, Connecticut, where he served until his death in 1879)

Note: Fort Adams had no permanent garrison during this period and was in caretaker status.

Civil War (1861–1866)

Note: Mayor Cranston of Newport placed a guard at Fort Adams at the request of the War Department in early January 1861.

COL (RI Militia) William Swan, Non-MA '33, CAN, April 19, 1861–May 8, 1861 (commanding officer of the "Old Guard" of the Artillery

APPENDIX A

Company of Newport; commanded the Artillery Company of Newport in the Dorr Rebellion of 1842)
Fort Adams served as United States Naval Academy, May 9, 1861–September 20, 1861 (Captain George Blake, USN, was superintendent)
Ordnance Sergeant Mark W. Smith, September 21, 1861–October 13, 1862 (Smith reenlisted at Fort Adams on December 12, 1863, and transferred on December 26 to Fort Trumbull, Connecticut)

Note: The fort was possibly under the command of Captain Charles W. Turner of the Newport Artillery Company during the preceding time frame.

LTC John P. Sanderson, Non-MA '61, 15th Inf., October 14, 1862–May 6, 1863
COL Oliver L. Shepherd, '40, 15th Inf., May 7, 1863–August 31, 1863
BG Robert Anderson, '25, September 1, 1863–September 21, 1863 (retired; was commanding officer at Fort Sumter, South Carolina, at the beginning of the Civil War; brevetted to major general on March 15, 1865)
COL (Brevet BG) Oliver L. Shepherd, '40, 15th Inf., September 22, 1863–March 14, 1866

POST–CIVIL WAR (1866–1899)

MAJ Joseph Stewart, '42, 4th, March 15, 1866–June 2nd, 1866
CPT (Brevet MAJ) George P. Andrews, '45, 3rd, June 3, 1866–July 28, 1866
COL (Brevet MG) Thomas W. Sherman, '36, 3rd, August 23, 1866–February 28, 1869 (commonly known as "the Other Sherman," he was a brigadier general of Volunteers during the Civil War; born in Newport and buried at the Island Cemetery)
COL (Brevet BG) Henry S. Burton, '39, 5th, March 1, 1869–April 4, 1869 (died)
Probably CPT (Brevet COL) Francis L. Guenther, '59, April 5, 1869–May 19, 1869 (interim)
COL (Brevet MG) Henry J. Hunt, '39, 5th, May 20, 1869–February 23, 1872 (brigadier general of Volunteers during the Civil War; served

APPENDIX A

as chief of artillery for the Army of the Potomac at the Battle of Gettysburg; stationed at Fort Adams from 1842 to 1843)
CPT Wallace F. Randolph, Non-MA '61, 5th, February 24, 1872–March 23, 1872 (interim)
CPT Henry A. DuPont, '61, 5th, March 24, 1872–May 22, 1872
COL (Brevet MG) Henry J. Hunt, '39, 5th, May 23, 1872–October 13, 1875
CPT Wallace F. Randolph, Non-MA '61, 5th, October 14, 1875–December 11, 1875
COL (Brevet BG) Israel Vogdes, '37, 1st, December 12, 1875–January 1, 1881 (brigadier general of Volunteers during the Civil War)
COL (Brevet BG) Fredrick T. Dent, '43, 1st, January 2, 1881–May 26, 1882 (brigadier general of Volunteers during the Civil War; Colonel Dent was on sick leave during this time, and operational command was assumed by Captain Taylor)
CPT (Brevet MAJ) Franck E. Taylor, Non-MA '61, 1st, January 2, 1881–January 9, 1882
CPT John W. Roder, Non-MA '62, 4th, January 9, 1882–February 8, 1882
CPT Henry C. Hasbrouck, '61, 4th, February 9, 1882–May 26, 1882
COL (Brevet MG) Albion P. Howe, '41, 4th, May 27, 1882–July 1, 1882 (retired; brigadier general of Volunteers during the Civil War)
CPT Henry C. Hasbrouck, '61, 4th, July 2, 1882–August 31, 1882 (interim)
CPT George B. Rodney, Non-MA '61, 4th, as of September 16, 1882–as of December 16, 1882
CPT (Brevet MAJ) Charles B. Throckmorton, Non-MA '61, 4th, September 12, 1882–
CPT (Brevet MAJ) John W. Roder, Non-MA '62, 4th, as of May 31, 1883
Possibly CPT (Brevet MAJ) Charles B. Throckmorton, Non-MA '61, 4th, as of June 9, 1883–November 15, 1883
COL Clermont L. Best, '47, 4th, November 16, 1883–April 25, 1888
CPT Edward Field, Non-MA '61, 4th, April 26, 1888–June 13, 1888 (interim)
COL Henry W. Closson, '47, 4th, June 14, 1888–May 24, 1889
COL John Mendenhall, '51, 2nd, May 27, 1889–June 18, 1892 (died on July 1, 1892)
CPT (Brevet MAJ) Harry C. Cushing, Non-MA '61, 2nd, June 19, 1892–August 2, 1892 (interim; veteran of Battery A, 1st RI Light Artillery in Civil War)

Appendix A

COL Richard Lorder, '56, 2nd, August 3, 1892–September 29, 1896 (retired)
CPT George Mitchell, '62, 2nd, September 30, 1896–November 30, 1896
COL Alexander C.M. Pennington, '60, 2nd, December 1, 1896–May 24, 1898 (promoted to brigadier general of Volunteers on May 4, 1898)
LTC William L. Haskin, Non-MA '61, 2nd, May 25, 1898–June 14, 1898
COL John G. Eddy, 47th NY Vol. Inf., June 15, 1898–October 11, 1898
LTC William L. Haskin, Non-MA '61, 2nd, October 12, 1898–November 23, 1898
CPT Sydney W. Taylor, Non-MA '67, 4th, November 24, 1898–February 26, 1899
CPT James C. Bush, '75, 7th, February 27, 1899–March 29, 1899

Early Twentieth Century (1899–1919)

CPT John A. Lundeen, '73, 7th, March 30, 1899–June 11, 1899
COL Henry C. Hasbrouck, '61, 7th, June 12, 1899–January 5, 1903

Note: All artillery units were redesignated as the Artillery Corps (AC) on February 13, 1901.

MAJ John P. Wisser, '74, AC, January 6, 1903–May 27, 1903 (interim)
COL William P. Ennis, '64, AC, May 28, 1903–November 6, 1905 (retired the next day as a brigadier general; buried at Island Cemetery in Newport)
CPT Millard F. Harmon, '80, AC, November 7, 1905–November 22, 1905 (interim; father of LTG Millard F. Harmon Jr. of the U.S. Army Air Corps, who died in the Pacific Theater in 1945; the younger Harmon may have lived at Fort Adams at this time)
CPT Henry D. Todd, Jr., '90, AC, November 22–November 27, 1905 (interim)
COL Louis V. Caziarc, Non-MA '64, AC, November 28, 1905–September 30, 1906
COL Walter Howe, '67, AC, October 1906–November 7, 1909 (promoted to brigadier general in 1910)

Appendix A

Note: On May 31, 1907, the Coast Artillery Corps (CAC) was established.

MAJ Samuel Kephart, CAC, November 8–December 16, 1909 (interim)
COL William Coffin, '73, CAC, December 17, 1909–July 8, 1912
MAJ Joseph P. Tracey, '96, CAC, July 9, 1912–November 14, 1912 (interim; received the Distinguished Service Medal in World War I)
COL Millard F. Harmon, '80, CAC, November 15, 1912–July 6, 1913
COL Charles H. Hunter, '80, CAC, July 7, 1913–October 31, 1913 (retired)
CPT William F. Stewart Jr., Non-MA '98, CAC, November 1, 1913–December 13, 1913 (interim)
COL George F. Landers, '87, CAC, December 14, 1913–August 13, 1915
COL Henry C. Davis, '83, CAC, August 1915–May 1916
LTC John C. Gilmore Jr., '94, CAC, September 14, 1915–May 9, 1917 (in command of Harbor Defenses of Narragansett Bay from May 1916 to February 1917)
COL Charles L. Phillips, '81, CAC, circa May 1916–May 9, 1917 (senior officer at Fort Adams; promoted to brigadier general during World War I)
MAJ Robert F. MacMillan, Non-MA '98, CAC, May 10, 1917–June 22, 1917 (interim)
COL Henry D. Todd Jr., '90, CAC, June 23, 1917–August 23, 1917 (interim; promoted to brigadier general on August 5, 1917; awarded the Distinguished Service Medal for service in World War I)
LTC Francis Cannon, CAC, RING, August 24, 1917–September 8, 1917
COL Oscar L Straub, '87, CAC, September 9, 1917–June 28, 1919

Fort Commanders (1915–1941)

Note: During this period, the U.S. Army distinguished between the officer in command of Harbor Defenses of Narragansett Bay and the commander of Fort Adams. This understanding may clear up seeming discrepancies in the list.

MAJ John C. Gilmore Jr., '94, CAC, as of November 1915
?, 1915–1919

Appendix A

MAJ Stephen H. Mould, Non-MA '98, CAC, as of October 24, 1919–circa 1920
MAJ Joseph J. Grace, '04, CAC, as of October 24, 1920
?, November 1920–June 1921 (probably Major Grace)
MAJ James W. Lyon, '08, CAC, June–August 1921 (interim)
MAJ Theodore Murphy, Non-MA '11, CAC, August 1921–circa 1923
MAJ Claude M. Thiele, Non-MA '11, CAC, circa 1923–October 14, 1926
CPT Ernest R. Barrows, Non-MA '08, 10th CA, October 15, 1926–February 2, 1927
?, February 1927–August 1928
Probably MAJ Robert Eddy, ?, 10th CA, August 1928–September 1928
CPT Ernest R. Barrows, Non-MA '08, 10th CA, September 1928–July 19, 1930
MAJ John P. Smith, Non-MA '08, 10th CA, July 20, 1930–October 30, 1930
MAJ Edward B. Dennis, Non-MA '10, 10th CA, November 1, 1930–October 1933
MAJ Carl Adams, Non-MA '17, 10th CA, October 1933–September 1936 (served as an enlisted soldier from 1911 to 1917)
LTC Paul H. Herman, Non-MA '09, 13th Inf., circa September 1936–August 1937
MAJ Edward L. Supple, Non-MA '07, 10th CA, August 1937–September 1937 (interim)
?, September 1937–November 1939
MAJ Ephriham P. Jolls, Non-MA '18, 10th CA, November 1939–March 26, 1940
MAJ George W. Brent, Non-MA '17, 10th CA, March 27, 1940–as of July 12, 1940

Interwar Period (1919–1939)

COL George F. Landers, '87, CAC, June 28, 1919–July 5, 1921
COL William A. Doores, Non-MA '98, CAC, July 6, 1921–October 27, 1923
LTC Samuel G. Shartle, Non-MA '99, 10th CA, October 28, 1923–October 6, 1926

Appendix A

Note: The 10th Coast Artillery Regiment was organized at Fort Adams on June 30, 1924.

CPT Fredric W. Cook, Non-MA '09, 10th CA, as of November 5, 1926 (interim; served as a colonel in World War I; graduated from Brown in 1905)
?, November 1926–February 1927
COL Thomas F. Dwyer, '95, 10th CA, February 3, 1927–August 9, 1927
COL James F. Brady, '97, 10th CA, August 10, 1927–January 26, 1928
LTC William H. Raymond, Non-MA '99, 10th CA, probably January 27, 1928–March 13, 1928
COL Hugh K. Taylor, Non-MA '99, 10th CA, March 14, 1928–as of July 31, 1928
COL Harold E. Cloke, ?, probably 10th CA, circa August 1928
COL Walter S. Grant, '00, 3rd Cav., as of July 6, 1929
COL Fredrick V.S. Chamberlain, Non-MA '98, 13th Inf., August 9, 1929–June 19, 1931
LTC John Scott, Non-MA '01 (?), 13th Inf. (?), June 20, 1931–circa July 1931
COL Albert W. Foreman, Non-MA '98, 13th Inf., as of July 1931–September 16, 1931
?, November 12, 1931–June 1932 (possibly MAJ Edward B. Dennis, Non-MA '10, 10th CA)
LTC Edward E. McCammon, '03 (?), 13th Inf., as of June 1932–June 28, 1934
LTC Fredrick C. Test, '05, 13th Inf., June 29, 1934–as of September 20, 1935
?, September 21–November 5, 1935
LTC Charles A. King Jr., '13, 13th Inf., as of November 5, 1935–May 31, 1936
COL Eugene Santschi, Non-MA '07, 13th Inf., June 1, 1936–December 15, 1936
COL Jere H. Baxter, Non-MA '07, 13th Inf., December 16, 1936–circa 1937
LTC Martin C. Schallenberger, Non-MA circa '15, 13th Inf., September 1–September 19, 1937
COL Paul H. Herman, Non-MA '09, 10th CA, September 20, 1937–as of July 1, 1938
COL Jere Baxter, Non-MA '07, 13th Inf., as of July 8, 1938–August 31, 1939

Appendix A

World War II (1939–1946)

LTC Thomas H. Jones, Non-MA '18, 10th CA, September 1, 1939–May 1940 (graduated from the Naval Academy in 1909 and served in the U.S. Navy until 1918; he was promoted to brigadier general in July 1941)
LTC Randolph T. Pendleton, Non-MA '11, 10th CA, May 1940–September 21, 1940
COL Earl C. Webster, Non-MA '18, 243rd CA, RING, September 22, 1940–March 5, 1941 (commanding officer of the 243rd Coast Artillery Regiment, Rhode Island National Guard; transferred to Fort Getty; discharged from active duty on December 12, 1941)
BG Ralph E. Haines, Non-MA '10, March 6, 1941–December 13, 1941
BG Thomas H. Jones, Non-MA '18, December 14–18, 1941 (interim)
BG Arthur G. Campbell, Non-MA '08, December 19, 1941–October 1943
COL Christopher D. Peirce, Non-MA '10, 10th CA, October 1943–February 21, 1946

Note: The 10th Coast Artillery Regiment was disbanded on February 25, 1944.

Final Years (1946–1950)

COL Earl H. Metzger, Non-MA '12, CA, February 22, 1946–August 31, 1949 (retired)
COL Edward B. McCarthy, Non-MA '17, CA, September 1, 1949–April 14, 1950 (reassigned as commander of Fort Devens, Massachusetts)
MAJ B.H. Schimmell, Non-MA ?, CA, April 15–May 31, 1950

Note: Fort Adams was deactivated as a Coast Artillery post on May 31, 1950, when the Coast Artillery Corps was disbanded. Also note that the 1950 Newport city directory lists Captain Lewis E. Denton as being assigned to Fort Adams. He was possibly in charge of disposing of surplus property at the fort.

APPENDIX A

1112TH ARMY SERVICE UNIT (1949–1952)

The 1112th Army Service Unit (ASU), "Narragansett Bay Marine Repair Shop," was stationed at Fort Adams from its organization on November 20, 1949, until June 30,1952. The unit's mission was maintaining and operating army watercraft in the Newport area. This was the last active army unit to be stationed at Fort Adams. Commanding officers of the 1112th ASU were as follows.

LTC George G. Trahey, TC, November 20, 1949–July 31, 1951
MAJ Orson L. Reeve, TC, August 1, 1951–June 30, 1952

APPENDIX B
UNITS STATIONED AT FORT ADAMS

The army units stationed at Fort Adams over the years were numerous and diverse. The information was obtained from a variety of sources, including official records, newspaper articles, privately published listings of military organizations and Newport city directories. For units in the early twentieth century, a list of Coast Artillery companies compiled by Bolling W. Smith of the Coast Defense Study Group was invaluable. For units at the fort during the Second World War, Walter Schroeder's *Defenses of Narragansett Bay in World War II* was consulted. Question marks (?) indicate where a date could not be found.

OLD FORT ADAMS (1799–1821)

Captain Henry's Company, 2nd Regiment Artillerists and Engineers, July 4, 1799–circa March 1802
Not garrisoned, 1802–1814
Wood's State Corps, Rhode Island Militia, July 1814–February 28, 1815
Light Artillery
    Captain Peyton's Company, as of January 1816
    Company G, March 1816–November 1819

Appendix B

Company D, January 1820–May 1820
Company I, May 1820–May 1821

Note: The fort was placed on caretaking status in 1821, and construction of the new Fort Adams began in 1825. The new fort was not garrisoned until the arrival of two companies of the 2nd Artillery in August 1841.

1841–1862

2nd Artillery
  Company F, August 1841–August 1843
  Company I, August 1841–August 1843
  Company E, May 1842–June 1842
  Company G, May 1842–June 1842
  Company A, July 1842–August 1843
1st Artillery
  Company K, July 1842–August 1845
  Company I, September 1843–August 1845
  Company F, September 1843–July 1845
2nd Artillery
  Company H, August 1845–September 1846
9th Infantry, April–May 1847 (the 9th Infantry Regiment used Fort Adams as a mobilization site prior to being shipped to Mexico)
3rd Artillery
  Headquarters, September 1848–July 1853
  Company B, September 1848–April 1849, May 1849–September 1849, June 1853–August 1853
  Company D, September 1848–September 1849
  Company E, January 1849–June 1853
  Company H, November 1848–September 1849, December 1850–September 1853
  Company L, September 1848–September 1849, December 1850–August 1853
  Company I, 1st Artillery, May 29, 1857–October 31, 1859

Appendix B

Civil War (1861–1866)

At the outbreak of the Civil War, Fort Adams was in caretaking status. The "Old Guard" of the Artillery Company of Newport garrisoned the fort from April to May 1861 when the U.S. Naval Academy was located at the fort. The Naval Academy moved to the Atlantic House hotel in Newport in September 1861. It is possible that the Artillery Company of Newport garrisoned the fort from September 1861 to October 1862, but documentation to support this hypothesis has not been found.

15th Infantry
   Headquarters and recruiting depot, October 1862–March 1866
   2nd and 3rd Battalions, October 1862–March 1866

Note: The 15th Infantry Regiment was organized into three battalions of eight companies each. The first battalion was organized prior to the 15th Infantry establishing its regimental headquarters and recruiting depot at Fort Adams in 1862. The 2nd and 3rd Battalions formed more slowly than anticipated with the result that companies of the 15th Infantry were still being recruited at the end of the Civil War. The 15th Infantry departed Fort Adams on March 15, 1866. In 1866, the 2nd and 3rd Battalions of the 15th Infantry were used to form two other infantry regiments.

Post–Civil War (1866–1901)

3rd Artillery
   Headquarters, June 1866–February 1869
   Company B, November 1865–February 1869
   Company D, April 1866–February 1869
   Company H, March 1866–February 1869
5th Artillery
   Headquarters, February 1869–December 1875
   Battery A, January 1869–November 1875
   Battery B, February 1869–December 1875
   Light Battery F, July 1870–November 1875
   Battery L, August 1870–December 1875

Appendix B

1st Artillery
 Headquarters, December 1875–December 1881
 Battery B, December 1875–1876, 1877–December 1881
 Battery E, December 1875–December 1881
 Battery F, December 1875–December 1881
 Battery K, December 1875–December 1881
4th Artillery
 Headquarters, November 1881–May 1889
 Light Battery B, Novmeber 1881–November 1896
 Battery D, November 1881–May 1889
 Battery E, November 1881–May 1889
 Battery L, November 1881–May 1889
 Battery G, September 1882–May 1889
2nd Artillery
 Headquarters, May 1889–November 1898
 Battery B, September 1895–November 1898
 Battery C, May 1889–September 1895
 Battery D, September 1895–November 1898
 Battery F, November 1896–April 1898
 Battery G, May 1889–March 1898
 Battery H, May 1889–April 1892
 Battery M, April 1892–September 1895
47th New York Volunteer Infantry Regiment, June 1898–October 1898 (the regiment was then transferred to Puerto Rico for occupation duty)
4th Artillery, Battery F, August 1898–as of March 1899
7th Artillery
 Headquarters, June 1899–February 1901.
 Battery A, December 1898–October 1899
 Battery C, June 1899–as of May 1900
 Battery H, May 1898–June 1898, August 1898–February 1901 (redesignated as 78th Co. CAC in February 1901)
 Battery I, June 1899–1901 (redesignated as 79th Co. CAC in February 1901)

Appendix B

1901–1917

In 1901, the artillery units of the army underwent a major reorganization. Instead of the traditional organization by regiment, the artillery units were divided into individual companies under the Artillery Corps. In 1907, the Artillery Corps was divided into the Coast Artillery Corps (CAC) and the Field Artillery, with the companies being assigned individually. This was in recognition of the reality that artillery regiments rarely operated as complete units, and their companies were usually dispersed to meet operational requirements. The regimental organization was restored for Field Artillery units when the United States entered World War I in 1917. Coast Artillery regiments were not established until 1924.

78th Co. CAC, organized in February 1901 from Co. H, 7th Artillery (transferred to Fort Moultrie in May 1907)
79th Co. CAC, organized in February 1901 from Co. I, 7th Artillery (transferred to Fort Monroe in May 1907)
97th Co. CAC, organized in July 1901 at Fort Adams (redesignated as 1st Co., Fort Adams in April 1917)
110th Co. CAC, September 1901–1910, when it was assigned to Fort Greble, Rhode Island (redesignated as 3rd Co., Fort Greble in 1916)
11th Battery, Field Artillery, September 1905–August 1906
102nd Co. CAC, May 1907–1916 (redesignated as 4th Co., Fort Adams in April 1917)
117th Co. CAC, May 1907–after December 1913
129th Co. CAC, August 1907–April 1917 (redesignated as 3rd Co., Fort Adams)
130th Co. CAC, August 1907–April 1917 (redesignated as 4th Co., Fort Adams)
38th Co. CAC, after December 1913–1916 (redesignated as 5th Co., Fort Adams in April 1917)

Appendix B

World War I (1917–1918)

When the Untied States declared war on Germany in April 1917, Coast Artillery companies were redesignated with the names of the fort at which they were located (e.g., 1st Co., Fort Adams).

Garrison of Fort Adams as of April 1917

1st Co. Fort Adams, organized in 1901 as 97th CA Company (redesignated as 1st Co., Fort Adams in April 1917)
2nd Co. Fort Adams, organized in 1901 as 117th CA Company (redesignated as 2nd Co., Fort Adams in April 1917; redesignated as Co. K, 7th Provisional CA Regiment, in July 1917; shipped overseas)
3rd Co. Fort Adams, organized in 1907 as 129th CA Company (redesignated as 3rd Co., Fort Adams in April 1917)
4th Co. Fort Adams, organized in 1907 as 130th CA Company (redesignated as 4th Co., Fort Adams in April 1917)
5th Co. Fort Adams, organized in 1901 as 102nd CA Company (redesignated as 5th Co., Fort Adams in April 1917)
Artillery Engineer Company, Fort Adams, Rhode Island, organized in 1917 (redesignated as 2nd Co., CD Narragansett Bay in 1918)

Units Organized at Fort Adams During the First World War

1st Expeditionary Brigade, consisting of 6th, 7th and 8th Provisional Coast Artillery Regiments, organized at Fort Adams in July 1917, shipped overseas in August 1917, redesignated as the 1st Separate Brigade in September 1917, redesignated as 30th Separate Artillery Brigade (Railway) in March 1918; returned to United States and demobilized in January 1919 (the 7th, 8th and 9th Regiments were redesignated as the 51st, 52nd and 53rd Regiments in February 1918 and served overseas

APPENDIX B

until early 1919, when they were returned to the United States and demobilized).

34th Artillery Brigade, organized at Fort Adams in February 1918 and shipped overseas July 1918; returned to United States and demobilized in February 1919.

66th Coast Artillery Regiment, organized at Fort Adams in March 1918 and shipped overseas in July 1918; returned to the United States and demobilized in March 1919.

7th Battalion, United States Guards, consisting of four companies, mobilized at Fort Adams in June 1918; its companies were assigned to duties in Massachusetts and Connecticut in October 1918; the battalion was demobilized in December 1918 at Camp Devens, Massachusetts.

INTERWAR YEARS (1919–1940)

After the armistice was signed on November 11, 1918, the U.S. Army was rapidly demobilized. As of January 11, 1919, five Coast Artillery companies were assigned to Fort Adams. They were the 1st, 2nd, 3rd, 5th and 6th Companies of the Coast Defenses of Narragansett Bay (CDNB). Other companies in the CDNB were distributed as follows: 24th at Fort Getty; 4th, 7th and 8th at Fort Greble; 25th at Fort Kearny; and the 23rd at Fort Wetherill.

1st Co. Narragansett Bay, assigned to Fort Adams as of January 11, 1919; redesignated as 97th Coast Artillery Company in 1922; redesignated as Battery A, 10th Coast Artillery Regiment (inactive), on July 1, 1924.

2nd Co. Narragansett Bay, assigned to Fort Adams as of January 11, 1919; redesignated as the 173rd Coast Artillery Company in 1922; redesignated as the Headquarters Battery of the 10th Coast Artillery Regiment on July 1, 1924.

3rd Co. Narragansett Bay, assigned to Fort Adams as of January 11, 1919; redesignated at 129th Coast Artillery Company in 1922; redesignated as Battery D, 10th Coast Artillery Regiment (inactive), on July 1, 1924.

5th Co. Narragansett Bay, assigned to Fort Adams as of January 11, 1919; redesignated as 110th Coast Artillery Company in 1922;

redesignated as Battery C, 10th Coast Artillery Regiment (inactive), on July 1, 1924.

6th Co. Narragansett Bay, assigned to Fort Adams as of January 11, 1919; consolidated with 5th Co. CDNB later in 1919.

10th Coast Artillery Regiment, constituted on July 1, 1924, and assigned to the HDNB and Harbor Defenses of New Bedford, Massachusetts; only the regimental headquarters was active, and subordinate units were "paper" units, which could be mobilized in the event of war.

13th Infantry Regiment

Headquarters and Band, September 22, 1928–September 17, 1931

2nd Battalion (consisting of the Battalion Headquarters and Companies E, F, G and H), September 22, 1928–October 21, 1939.

WORLD WAR II (1940–1945)

Harbor Defenses of Narragansett Bay (HDNB) was the overall headquarters of all coast defense posts and units in Rhode Island; it served throughout World War II. There were several reorganizations of the HDNB during the war as the number of personnel and units in the HDNB were reduced to reflect the decreased threat to the continental United States and the need for more personnel to be sent overseas.

10th Coast Artillery Regiment, activated on April 1, 1940. It consisted of the regimental headquarters and four Coast Artillery batteries (A through D) organized into two battalions. As of December 1943, the regiment had expanded to seven companies (A through G) and was dispersed at various locations in Narragansett Bay. Only the regimental headquarters was at Fort Adams. The regiment was disbanded on February 25, 1944, and its surplus personnel were reassigned.

243rd Coast Artillery Regiment (Rhode Island National Guard), inducted into federal service on September 16, 1940, and moved to Fort Adams on September 22, 1940. The regimental headquarters was moved to Fort Getty in Jamestown on March 14, 1941, where it served under Narragansett Bay Harbor Defenses. As of December 1943, the regiment had nine batteries, of which only one, Battery H, was located at Fort Adams. Battery H manned three 75mm antiaircraft

APPENDIX B

guns (later replaced by two 90mm antiaircraft guns) at the fort. The 243rd Coast Artillery Regiment was reorganized on October 7, 1944, intothe 188th and 189th Coast Artillery battalions with four and three companies, respectively.

188th and 189th Battalions, consolidated into a single battalion of four companies under HDNB on April 1, 1945.

701st Anti-Aircraft Artillery Gun Battalion (semi-mobile), organized under HDNB on September 1, 1943. It was reassigned to the Replacement and School Command on October 25, 1944.

POST–WORLD WAR II

Information on the units assigned to Fort Adams after the end of World War II is lacking. It is known, however, that Fort Adams was commanded by a senior officer, with the rank of colonel, as late as April 14, 1950, six weeks before the disbanding of the Army Coast Artillery Corps on May 31 of the same year. This would indicate that Fort Adams still was home to a Coast Artillery district headquarters from 1945 to 1950.

The last army unit at Fort Adams was the 1112th Army Service Unit, which served at the fort from November 20, 1949, to June 30, 1952. This unit maintained army watercraft associated with air defenses in the Rhode Island area. It was probably also responsible for disposing of surplus property at the fort.

REFERENCES

Order of Battle of the United States Land Forces in the World War. Vol. 3, parts 1 and 2. Washington, D.C.: Center of Military History, United States Army, 1988.

———. Vol. 3, part 3. Washington, D.C.: Center of Military History, United States Army, 1988, 1,164–1,167, 1,190–1,191, 1,566.

Returns from Military Posts, 1806–1916. United States Army, Adjutant General. Available online at Ancestry.com.

Schroeder, Walter K. *Defenses of Narragansett Bay in World War II.* Providence: Rhode Island Publications Society, 1980, 120–22.

Smith, Bolling W. *Coast Artillery Companies, 1901–1924.* Coast Defense Reference Guide. Coast Defense Study Group, 433–55. http://cdsg.org/old/reprint%20PDFs/CACcomp.pdf.

United States Army Order of Battle, 1919–1941. Vol. 2. Editd by Lieutenant Colonel (Ret.) Steven E. Clay. Fort Leavenworth, KS: Combat Studies Institute Press, n.d., 1,066–1,067.

FORT ADAMS HALL OF FAME

Joseph G. Totten—Oversaw construction of Fort Adams; served twenty-five years as chief engineer of the United States Army.

Louis Tousard—French military engineer who oversaw construction of Old Fort Adams.

Alexander McGregor—Scottish stonemason who constructed Fort Adams.

Maudie Allen—Long-serving hostess at the service club at Fort Adams.

Robert Anderson—Commander of Fort Sumter at the start of the Civil War; briefly commanded Fort Adams in 1863.

John Henry—First commander of Fort Adams; instrumental in the United States' declaring war on Great Britain in 1812.

Mark W. Smith—Served more than fifty years in the U.S. Army until his death at age seventy-six; ordnance sergeant at Fort Adams for several years.

John B. Magruder—Confederate general who commanded Fort Adams; noted for his hopitality and flamboyant personality.

Henry A. DuPont—Member of the DuPont family and West Point graduate who received the Medal of Honor; stationed at Fort Adams after the Civil War and later was a United States senator.

Ambrose Burnside—Civil War general, governor of Rhode Island and United States senator.

Thomas W. Sherman—Newport native who distinguished himself during the Civil War; commanded Fort Adams after the war.

Pierre G.T. Beauregard—Engineer during the construction of Fort Adams; commander of Confederate forces that attacked Fort Sumter in April 1861.

Appendix B

John G. Barnard—Noted American military engineer; worked as engineer during construction of Fort Adams.

Simon G. Bernard—Designer of Fort Adams and military engineer for Napoleon; brought advanced military engineering techiques to the United States.

Henry Jackson Hunt—Union artillery commander at the Battle of Gettysburg; commanded Fort Adams after the war.

William Gates—Long-serving U.S. Army officer; commanded Fort Adams.

Robley D. Evans—At Fort Adams as a cadet with the U.S. Naval Academy in 1861; rose to rear admiral and commander the first leg of the Great White Fleet's around-the-world voyage in 1907.

Charles V. Gridley—At Fort Adams as a cadet with the U.S. Naval Academy in 1861; commander of the USS *Olympia* at the Battle of Manila Bay.

George Uhle—Medal of Honor recipient.

Franklin Pierce—Briefly commanded Fort Adams; brigadier general in the Mexican-American War and later president of the United States.

Truman B. Ransom—Commander of the 9th Infantry Regiment in Mexico; killed in action.

John S. Slocum—In the 9th Infantry during the Mexican-American War and was at Fort Adams with the regiment prior to going to Mexico; served as the colonel of the 2nd Rhode Island at the Battle of Bull Run in July 1861, where he was killed in action.

APPENDIX C
THE ARTILLERY OF FORT ADAMS

Introduction

The purpose of this appendix is to give the reader a basic understanding of the number and types of artillery pieces at Fort Adams over the years. As this is an exceedingly broad and complex subject, only a very general overview can be provided here

Old Fort Adams (1799–1821)

When Old Fort Adams was dedicated on July 4, 1799, it was armed with twelve 32-pounder cannons. (The designation means that the cannons fired a cannonball weighing 32 pounds.) Later, in 1811, an official army report lists the fort's armament as seventeen guns but does not specify their sizes. A reasonable assumption would be that the twelve 32s remained and five more cannons were added.

In 1821, Old Fort Adams was deactivated, and construction of the new fort began in 1824. By 1841, the construction had advanced to the point that the fort was garrisoned, and Fort Adams was again an active coast defense fort.

New Fort Adams (1841–1865)

In the 1840s, Fort Adams was probably equipped with 24-pounders instead of the flank howitzers. This is because the flank howitzers did not go into production until 1844, and the carronade was well adapted for short-range anti-personnel work. Additional evidence is provided by a drawing of a carronade at Fort Adams in 1835 in the book *Roundshot and Rammers* (Stackpole Books, 1969) by Harold L. Peterson.

The earliest armament return of Fort Adams, discovered so far, is from 1854 and shows Fort Adams being armed with one hundred 32-pounders, fifty-seven 24-pounders and forty-three 24-pounder flank howitzers (see the *American State Papers*, vol. 17).

This armament remained virtually unchanged until the Civil War. In January 1862, the fort had an armament of 100 32-pounders (5 mounted en barbette and 18 in casemates), 56 24-pounders (16 mounted en barbette and 11 in casemates) and 43 24-pounder flank howitzers (9 mounted in casemates), as well as 2 6-pounder field guns, 2 12-pounder howitzers and 1 8-inch mortar, for a total of 204 guns. In addition to the guns mounted above, there were 48 carriages without guns mounted on them, according to the *Newport Mercury*, January 18, 1862.

Post–Civil War (1866–1897)

A report dated June 30, 1866, shows that shortly after the Civil War, the fort's armament underwent significant changes. Although most of the old antebellum cannons remained, they were supplemented by eleven massive 15-inch Rodmans (two mounted on the southwest bastion of the exterior front by 1873 and an additional three mounted south of the fort's exterior ditch by 1894), thirteen 10-inch Rodmans (ten

APPENDIX C

A 15-inch Rodman gun being fired. *National Archives/Daniel P. Titus Collection.*

being mounted in the center tier in the southernmost end of the west wall) and four 100-pounder Parrott rifles (mounted facing south in the northwest bastion).

These three types of guns formed the fort's major batteries from the end of the Civil War until 1898. The Parrott rifles were renowned for their long range and accuracy but were notorious for bursting after heavy use. From their south-facing position, they could cover the approach to Newport for miles out to sea and would probably be the first guns fired in the event a hostile fleet attacked Newport.

In the event of an attack, the 15-inch Rodmans would have been the fort's main batteries and would have concentrated their fire on the larger enemy ships. The 10-inch Rodmans would have taken care of any smaller vessels, as well as finishing off, at close range, any ships that survived the fire of the 15-inchers.

For mobile defense, Fort Adams was supplied with four 4.5-inch siege rifles. These were mounted on wheeled carriages and could be deployed anywhere necessary for the defense of the fort or the city of Newport.

By 1873, all of the old 24-pounders and all but twenty rifled 32-pounders had been removed from the fort. Also, four 3-inch Ordnance Rifles on field carriages and four 10-inch siege mortars model of 1861 had been added to the fort's armament.

Appendix C

The return of 1883 showed even more types of ordnance being sent to the fort. One 10-inch seacoast mortar model of 1861 and four 30-pounder Parrott rifles had been added. The Parrotts were probably replacements for the 4.5-inch siege rifles, as they had been dismounted from their carriages.

By July 1, 1894, four 8-inch converted rifles had been emplaced to the south of the main fort complex about where Battery Bankhead would be later located. (Converted rifles were made by inserting a rifled sleeve into a 10-inch Rodman gun to give it more range and accuracy.)

Endicott Period Batteries (1898–1916)

The "Endicott Period" refers to weapons developed as a result of the Endicott Board, which was established in 1885 to access the nation's coast defense needs. The primary findings of the board were that the country needed to build new fortifications armed with modern rifled breech-loading artillery pieces. The new weapons were a veritable quantum leap in firepower above the existing Civil War vintage artillery pieces then in service.

While the earliest Endicott batteries date from 1895, the first battery at Fort Adams was not commenced until 1897.

On February 15, 1898, the armored cruiser USS *Maine* blew up in Havana Harbor, and the United States was soon at war with Spain. This was untimely from the standpoint of coast defense, as the modern weapons of the Endicott system were in the process of being developed and emplaced; as a result, few ports in the country were protected by modern guns.

At the outbreak of the Spanish-American War, the two batteries of 12-inch mortars at Fort Adams (named Green and Edgerton) were nearing completion and would be operational later in the year. Each battery had eight mortars, for a total of sixteen. They were more than equal to any battleship afloat at that time and had a range of twelve thousand yards.

In addition to the mortars, an 8-inch breech-loading rifle was emplaced in one of the 15-inch Rodman emplacements to the south of the old fort complex. These were modern weapons mounted on the older carriages for the massive Rodmans. While the combining of the old and new may

Appendix C

A 12-inch mortar, Model 1890, at either Battery Greene or Battery Edgerton. The ring on the wall is for attaching ropes used to maneuver the mortars into place when they are installed. *John S. and Margaret D. Dugan Collection.*

Soldiers in dungaree uniforms fire 12-inch mortars at Fort Adams between 1898 and 1917. *National Archives/Daniel P. Titus Collection.*

Appendix C

Gun crew reloading a 6-inch disappearing rifle. *John S. and Margaret D. Dugan Collection.*

seem strange, it was a quick fix for the need for modern rapid-fire artillery pieces. The gun was removed in about 1900 and, presumably, installed at another fort.

Another report, dated December 31, 1899, shows that one 8-inch breech-loading rifle mounted on a 15-inch Rodman carriage had been emplaced near the battery of 8-inch converted rifles. The 8-inch breech-loading rifles were emplaced during the Spanish-American Wars as stopgap measures while more modern "disappearing" guns were being produced. A total of only twenty-three were emplaced.

Another weapon listed on the 1899 ordnance report is a 3.6-inch breech-loading mortar, Model of 1890. This was a rare artillery piece (only seventy-six were made) and was probably used to train gunners in the use of indirect fire weapons without incurring the expense of firing larger mortars.

In 1897, work began on the first of the new Endicott Period batteries. This was the mortar pit located south of the main fort. These emplacements,

Appendix C

Disappearing guns, probably at nearby Fort Wetherill, at the ready. *John S. and Margaret D. Dugan Collection.*

Early disappearing rifle. This photo was probably taken at Fort Hancock, New Jersey. *John S. and Margaret D. Dugan Collection.*

Appendix C

Above: A 10-inch disappearing rifle of Battery Reilly at Fort Adams ready to fire. *John S. and Margaret D. Dugan Collection.*

Opposite, top: Gatling guns near the Fort Adams hospital in about 1900. *John S. and Margaret D. Dugan Collection.*

Opposite, bottom: A 3-inch mine defense gun at Battery Belton in the early twentieth century. *John S. and Margaret D. Dugan Collection.*

named Batteries Greene and Edgerton, originally mounted a total of sixteen 12-inch breech-loading mortars that became operational on June 24, 1898—just in time for the Spanish-American War.

The mortars were supplemented the next year (1899) by two 4.72-inch Armstrong rifles at Battery Talbot and two 10-inch disappearing rifles at Battery Reilly. These weapons, supplemented by new batteries at Fort Wetherill in Jamestown, gave Narragansett Bay its first modern direct-fire weapons. With ranges of 11,800 and 15,000 yards, respectively, they greatly increased the effectiveness of the bay's defenses.

A report of the fort's ordnance dated December 31, 1902, states that the fort had two 6-pounder field guns. These were small, mobile guns to help defend the fort against attacking ground forces.

Appendix C

Appendix C

The Newport Artillery Company with a 3-inch field gun (Model 1902), early 1970s. *John S. and Margaret D. Dugan Collection.*

The old muzzleloading 10- and 15-inch Rodmans were removed from Fort Adams in 1902. These were followed by the 8-inch converted rifles in 1904. This marked the end of iron muzzleloading smoothbore cannons as part of American coast defense.

In 1907, Battery Belton, with two 3-inch mine defense guns (also called 15-pounders), and Battery Bankhead, with three 6-inch Armstrong rifles, were added, completing Fort Adams's modern armament. The 6-inch rifles had a range of fourteen thousand yards—almost eight miles.

First World War (1917–1918)

When the United States declared war on Germany in April 1917, most of the Endicott batteries at Fort Adams were still in service. It was quickly realized (as it was in both the Civil War and Spanish-American War) that there were no defenses to guard the east side of Aquidneck Island. In response, the two 4.72-inch guns of Battery Talbot were moved to Sachuest Point in Middletown.

APPENDIX C

A 10-inch gun of Battery Reilly being fired. *National Archives/Daniel P. Titus Collection.*

Loading a 10-inch disappearing gun at Battery Reilly in about 1900. *Fort Adams Trust.*

This battery covered the entrance of the Sakonnet River and provided an early warning station in the event of an approaching fleet. (In the days prior to radar and long-range aircraft, coastal watch stations were of great importance in detecting hostile fleets.) When the war concluded, the battery was deactivated, and the guns were declared obsolete in 1920. In 1923, one was put on display at Equality Park in Newport, where it remains to this day. The other was displayed at the Westerly, Rhode Island National Guard Armory until it was traded for an 8-inch Parrott rifle from Fort Moultrie in 1977.

APPENDIX C

These pieces are unique in that they are the only surviving guns documented to have armed Fort Adams, and they are possibly the only matched set of 4.72-inch Armstrong rifles known to be in existence. They are also the only two artillery pieces in existence that are authenticated to have been emplaced at Fort Adams.

Other batteries at Fort Adams were stripped to provide heavy artillery pieces for the U.S. Army in France. The 10-inch guns of Battery Reilly were removed, as were eight of the 12-inch mortars of Batteries Green and Edgerton.

INTERIM (1917–1938)

By the end of the First World War, only the eight 12-inch mortars and the two 3-inch guns of Battery Belton remained at Fort Adams. In 1925, Battery Belton was deactivated.

Sometime between the world wars, the fort had received three 3-inch Model 1917 antiaircraft guns. Two were emplaced on the outer front of the fort's redoubt (located south of the commanding officer's quarters) and the other between the redoubt and the commanding officer's quarters. They

Mortar reloading drill, circa 1920s. *National Archives/Daniel P. Titus Collection.*

APPENDIX C

A 12-inch gun at Fort Wetherill on a barbette mount. *John S. and Margaret D. Dugan Collection.*

The mobile 3-inch antiaircraft guns in this rare photo are probably mounted on Ford Model T chasses. *John S. and Margaret D. Dugan Collection.*

could fire at aircraft at altitudes up to 27,900 feet and reflected the changes in warfare that would dominate the Second World War. Photographic evidence indicates that, at some point, these guns were supplemented by at least two mobile M1918 antiaircraft guns. These guns were shorter than the M1917 and were mounted on either a trailer or, in the case of the guns at Fort Adams, the chassis of a Model T Ford.

Appendix C

World War II (1939–1945)

When World War II broke out in 1939, the only remaining major-caliber guns at Fort Adams were the eight 12-inch mortars at Batteries Greene and Edgerton. These were never activated during the war and were scrapped in 1942.

An 8-inch gun from a battery at Fort Church in Little Compton, Rhode Island, during World War II. *John S. and Margaret D. Dugan Collection.*

Appendix C

90mm Antiaircraft Gun

The 3-inch Model 1917 antiaircraft guns were replaced in 1944 by two M1 90mm antiaircraft guns, which could shoot at aircraft up to an altitude of 33,800 feet. The 90mm guns were also supplemented by 40mm antiaircraft guns, as well as .50-caliber machine guns. These were the last artillery pieces to arm Fort Adams and were removed sometime before the fort was deactivated in 1950.

Artillery Pieces Currently at Fort Adams

There are currently several artillery pieces at Fort Adams. This section will explain their history to the best of the authors' knowledge.

The 24-Pounder Guns

There are now at Fort Adams seven 24-pounder cannons (identified as such by both weight markings—one is clearly marked 50.1.0—and bore diameter) that apparently date from the late 1700s. Such dating is reasonable as the cannons lack markings indicating their date and place of manufacture, which was more common at later dates. They also lack trunnion bases, which indicates that they were probably manufactured before the War of 1812. They were definitely manufactured before 1819 as the Model 1819 24-pounder has trunnion bases and has a wide flange at the muzzle. Theories that the guns may be of British or French origin do not withstand scrutiny, as the guns lack distinguishing marking indicating manufacture in those countries.

These pieces were pulled out of the water near Fort Adams in the 1970s. It is possible that these pieces were part of the armament of Old Fort Adams and were disposed of after the new fort was armed in 1841. The old design of these pieces was superseded by the 1819 model of 24-pounders (examples of which can be seen at Fort Phoenix in Fairhaven, Massachusetts) and, therefore, would have been obsolete at that time. Another theory—which, unfortunately, cannot be proven—

is that they may have come from the famous frigate USS *Constitution* (aka "Old Ironsides"), which was moored at Fort Adams when the U.S. Naval Academy was located there in 1861.

It is possible that these seven guns are the largest surviving artillery pieces manufactured in the United States prior to 1800, as there are records of the Hope Furnace in Rhode Island receiving orders for this caliber of gun in 1794. Incidentally, these seven 24-pounders are identical in design, but not size, to the two 18-pounders at Stonington Village, Connecticut, that defended that town during the War of 1812, indicating that all of the pieces were probably produced around the same time and place.

The Constellation *Gun*

In the late 1990s, author John Duchesneau received an inquiry from the owner of a gun reputed to be from the sloop of war USS *Constellation* (now preserved in Baltimore), desiring to sell it. The *Constellation* was commissioned in 1854 and was the last ship in the navy to be propelled only by sails. The owner said that it was purchased at a navy surplus auction from the Newport Naval Station in the 1950s.

Investigation determined that the gun was an 8-inch shell gun and that guns of this type armed the *Constellation*. Furthermore, photos were found of a "battery" of four guns of this type, with an identical style of carriage, at the Newport Naval Station in the early twentieth century—the same era during which the *Constellation* was assigned to the Naval Station.

The author consulted the late Wayne Stark, who was the leading authority on Civil War–era artillery pieces. Mr. Stark's opinion was that the gun would be of minimal value on the collector's market. The author then suggested to the owner that he donate the gun to the Fort Adams Trust in order to qualify for a tax deduction. The gun was donated to the trust a few years later and is now located on the fort's parade ground.

The Replica 24-Pounder

Located near the redoubt/jail is a replica 24-pounder. Examination reveals that it is hollow and was cast in two pieces (upper and lower). This gun was located for many years on Memorial Boulevard in Newport near

Easton's Beach. A little-known fact is that it is actually from the famous frigate USS *Constitution*.

In about 1907, the *Constitution* was restored to its historic appearance after having its spar deck housed over for use as a barracks. It was quickly realized that there were no available authentic guns to put on the ship, and replica guns were made—presumably at the Boston Navy Yard. From 1927 to 1931, the *Constitution* underwent an extensive "from the keel up" restoration in Boston, and more authentic replica guns were made to "arm" it. The *Constitution* then went on a national goodwill tour during which the navy donated the original replica guns to the cities it visited. The gun Newport received is now on display at Fort Adams.

The East Gate Guns

In front of the fort's east gate are two replica guns. They were probably made in the early 1970s. Two other replicas of the same style are sunk in the ground as decorative pieces on Bowen's Wharf in Newport.

The 42-Pounder Carronade

While not located at Fort Adams, this piece is worth mentioning. It is located at the flagpole of Middletown High School and is reputed to be from the *Constitution*. A return of the fort's armament from 1902 mentions a "relic" carronade. As with the 24-pounder guns, it is possible that it was left at Fort Adams by the *Constitution*, but unfortunately, this cannot be proven with currently known sources.

CONCLUSION

During the course of Fort Adams's history, weaponry progressed from cannonballs to atomic bombs. As the world entered the late twentieth century, old forts were no longer needed, and the guns of Fort Adams quietly faded away as new weapons were developed to deal with the challenges of a new era in human history.

Appendix C

Armament of Fort Adams and Other Narragansett Bay Forts from 1898 through 1943

All data is from the Coast Defense Study Group Database (http://www.cdsg.org).

Fort Adams, Newport

Unnamed,1-8" Rod, 1898–circa 1900 (8" breech-loading rifle mounted on 15" Rodman carriage)
Greene, 8-12" mortar, 1898–1943 (renamed Battery Gilmore in World War II)
Edgerton, 8-12" mortar, 1898–1943
Reilly, 2-10" rifles on disappearing carriages, 1899–1917
Bankhead, 3-6" Armstrong rifles, 1907–13
Talbot, 2-4.72" Armstrong rifles, 1899–1917 (one 4.72" gun is in Equality Park, Newport; the other is at Fort Moultrie, South Carolina)
Belton, 2-3", pedestal mounts, 1907–25

Fort Church, Sakonnet Point (3 Sections)

Gray (#107), 2-16", CBC, 1942–48, West Reservation
Reilly, 2-8", CBC, 1942–47, East Reservation
#212, 2-6", SBC, 1943–48, South Reservation, Warren Point
Unnamed, 2-155mm, Panama mount

Fort Wetherill, Conanicut Island, 1900–1945

Varnum, 2-12", barbette carriage, 1901–43
Wheaton, 2-12", disappearing carriage, 1908–45
Walbach, 3-10", disappearing carriage, 1908–42
Zook, 3-6", disappearing carriage, 1908–18
Dickenson, 2-6", pedestal, 1908–47, modified in World War II
Crittenden, 2-3", pedestal, 1908–46
Cooke, 2-3", MP, 1901–20
AMTB 923, 2-90mm, fixed, circa 1943, modified old 3-in AA blocks

APPENDIX C

FORT GETTY, Conanicut Island, 1903

Tousard, 3-12", disappearing carriage, 1910–42
House, 2-6", pedestal, 1910–42, guns and carriages to Fort Varnum
Whiting, 2-3", pedestal, 1910–42, guns and carriages to Fort Burnside
Armistead (3), 2-3", pedestal, 1943, Whiting, emplacements, guns and carriages from Varnum
AMTB 922, 2-90mm, fixed, 1943–46

FORT BURNSIDE, Beavertail, 1940–1948

#110, 2-16", casemated, not built
#213, 2-6", fixed, 1943–48
Whiting (2), 2-3", pedestal, 1942–46

FORT GREBLE, Dutch Island, 1863

Sedgwick, 8-12", mortar, 1901–42
Hale, 3-10", disappearing carriages, 1898–1942
Mitchell, 3-6", pedestal, 1905–17
Mitchell, 1-6", Armstrong, 1898, gun to Fort Adams for Battery Bankhead
Ogden, 2-3", pedestal, 1900–1920

FORT KEARNY, Saunderstown, 1904

French, 4-6", disappearing carriages, 1908–17
Cram, 2-6", disappearing carriages, 1908–43
Armistead, 2-3", pedestal, 1908–42, guns and carriages to Fort Varnum

FORT VARNUM, Boston Neck, Narragansett, 1941

House (2), 2-6", pedestal, 1942–47, guns from Fort Getty
Armistead (2), 2-3", pedestal, 1942–43, guns from Fort Kearny, moved to Getty
AMTB 921, 2-90mm, fixed, 1943–46

Appendix C

Fort Greene, Point Judith (3 Sections)

Hamilton (#108), 2-16", casemated, 1943–48
#109, 2-16", casemated, 1944, never armed, West Reservation, guns were on site
#211, 2-6", fixed, 1945–48, South Reservation
Unnamed, 4-155mm, Panama Mount

Other Locations

Talbot, 2-4.7", A, 1917–19, Sachuest Point, guns were moved from Fort Adams
AMTB 924, 2-90mm, fixed, never built?
AMTB 923, 2-90mm, fixed, 1943?, Brenton Point, moved to Fort Wetherill
Unnamed, 4-155mm, Panama Mount, Brenton Point

References

American State Papers. "Military Affairs." Vols. 16–22.

"Armament Returns from Fort Adams." Available at the National Archives, Washington, D.C.

Coast Defense Study Group Database. www.cdsg.org. Lists all known coast defense batteries of the United States from 1885 through 1945.

Recommended Reading

Olmstead, Edwin, Wayne E. Stark and Spencer E. Tucker. *The Big Guns.* Alexandria Bay, NY: Museum Restoration Service, 1997. This is the most comprehensive book ever written about heavy artillery of the Civil War.

Appendix C

Peterson, Harold L. *Roundshot and Rammers: An Introduction to Muzzle-Loading Land Artillery in the United States.* N.p.: Bonanza Books, 1969. Contains general information about artillery prior to the 1870s.

Ripley, Warren. *Artillery and Ammunition of the Civil War.* N.p.: Promontory Press, 1973. A good general reference about the artillery of the Civil War.

Schroeder, Walter K. *Defenses of Narragansett Bay in World War II.* Rhode Island Publications Society, 1980.

NOTES

PART I

1. McBurney, *Rhode Island Campaign*, especially 1–21 and 70–95.
2. The earthwork held one eighteen-, one nine-, one six- and two four-pounder cannons. "Pounder" in artillery terminology indicates the weight of the shot, not of the gun.
3. Cullum, *Cullum's Historical Sketch*; Stiles, *Literary Diary of Ezra Stiles*, vol. 2.5.
4. Stiles, *Literary Diary of Ezra Stiles*, vol. 2.8.
5. All information in this paragraph is taken from McBurney, *Rhode Island Campaign*, especially chapters 5 through 8, 96–195.
6. The foregoing three paragraphs are adapted from Troost-Cramer, *True Tales of Life and Death*, 41–42, 108–9 (notes 51 and 52).
7. The former site of Fort Greene is now the small public park known as Battery Park, on Washington Street in the Point section of Newport.
8. This fort was also known as Fort Brown and/or Fort Dumplings, after the rocky terrain on which it was situated. The fort itself was a round tower, about fifty feet in diameter and about twenty feet in height. Never having seen action, it was employed more as a curiosity for artists than an active artillery emplacement, featuring in many nineteenth-century landscapes of Newport Harbor. In an official report dated December 11, 1818, "Fort Dumplings" was listed as being armed with ten guns, likely emplaced during the War of 1812. However, there is no evidence that the fort ever

figured in defense plans for Newport after that war or indeed that it was ever even garrisoned. There are no remains of Fort Dumplings today.
9. Begun in 1798, Fort Hamilton was never completed nor activated. However, the *Newport Mercury* in 1808 ran an advertisement on behalf of one Captain Baen of the Fourth U.S. Infantry offering a reward for a soldier who had deserted his company stationed on Rose Island. From the late 1800s to 1950, Rose Island served as part of the Naval Torpedo Station (the main part of which was located on Goat Island) and was used as a gun cotton storage facility. The island came into use by the military again during World War II, when antiaircraft guns were placed there. Today, Rose Island is owned by the Rose Island Lighthouse Foundation. The lighthouse, built in 1869, stands on the circular southwest bastion of Fort Hamilton. This, along with the northwest bastion and a row of stone barracks that were designed to house three hundred soldiers and were considered the finest in the young nation (according to the 1802 report of the U.S. secretary of war), are all that remain of that fortification.
10. For more on the planned defensive works for Narragansett Bay and its passages, see Robinson, "Fort Adams," 79.
11. *United States Military Reservations, etc.*, 356.
12. For more on Tousard's influence on the design of Narragansett Bay's defenses, see Robinson, "Fort Adams," 78.
13. *Newport Mercury,* July 9, 1799.
14. The artillery and engineer branches of the U.S. Army were united at this period in history. Captain Henry's company was the "ancestor" of the First Battalion of the Second Air Defense Artillery Regiment, which was an active unit in the U.S. Army as recently as 1991.
15. Adams, "Count Edward de Crillon."
16. Adams, *History of the United States of America*, 419–20. In "March 9, 1812: Henry's Papers Delivered to Congress" at http://1812now.blogspot.com/2012/03/march-9-1812-henrys-papers-delivered-to.html.
17. *American State Papers*, "Foreign Affairs," vol. 3, 545–54.
18. Adams, "Count Edward de Crillon," 52.
19. *Newport Mercury,* July 5, 1817.
20. *Congressional Serial Set*, No. 54, Section 98, 9–10.
21. This and the previous paragraph are adapted from Troost-Cramer, *True Tales of Life and Death*, 43.
22. For a more thorough discussion of Bernard and his broader career, see Robinson, "Fort Adams," 78, 80.

23. Totten would hold this position until his death in 1864, by which time he had attained the rank of brigadier general.
24. One of Totten's more familiar masterpieces is the Minot's Ledge Lighthouse near Scituate, Massachusetts. This lighthouse was under construction for five years, from 1855 to 1860, and is to this day considered one of the greatest engineering achievements of the nineteenth century. Minot's Ledge Lighthouse is still in active service today.
25. *Newport Mercury*, "Fort Adams Anniversary." The newspaper reports that the document had been placed in 1828, but the document itself states that the cornerstone was laid in 1825. Presumably, the document would have already been in the stone and therefore "1828" is likely a misprint.
26. The Perry Mill, built in 1835 at the corner of Thames Street and America's Cup Avenue, now houses retail and dining establishments. See http://wikimapia.org/21162073/Perry-Mill-1835-Newport-Bay-Club-Hotel.
27. The authors are indebted to Michael Slein, vice-president of the Museum of Newport Irish History, for this insight.
28. *Newport Mercury*, March 3, 1827; July 22, 1836.
29. See Troost-Cramer, *True Tales of Life and Death*, 60–62, 110 (notes 74–77).
30. Ibid.
31. For more on the fort's construction materials, see Robinson, "Fort Adams."
32. Troost-Cramer, *True Tales of Life and Death*, 57–58, 110 (notes 71 and 72).
33. Ibid., 57–60, 110 (note 73).
34. *Newport Mercury*, October 21, 1826.

PART II

35. During the Civil War, Captain Pitman served as lieutenant colonel of the First Rhode Island Detached Militia from May to August 1861.
36. Stevens's son, Hazard, who was born during his father's tenure at Fort Adams, would grow up to enter the army himself and earn the Medal of Honor with a brevetting to the rank of brigadier general.
37. This paragraph adapted from Troost-Cramer, *True Tales of Life and Death*, 81–82. For more on the deadly effectiveness of Fort Adams's design, see Robinson, "Fort Adams," 90–91.
38. Magruder also held the rank of brevet lieutenant colonel.
39. *Newport Mercury*, "Fort Adams."

40. "An Old Resident," "Fort Adams in 1858–61."
41. *Newport Daily News*, September 14, 1863.
42. Smith's cause of death was given as chronic diarrhea.
43. *Newport Mercury*, January 19, 1861.
44. Hills, "Mount Pleasant Almost Starts 'The War.'"
45. Ibid.
46. Ibid.
47. See Troost-Cramer, *True Tales of Life and Death*, 46, 48–49, 109 (note 59).
48. *Newport Mercury*, January 5, 1861. Ironically, despite the fort's bucolic environment, desertion was common.
49. Find a Grave, "Pierre Gustave Toutant Beauregard."
50. The Old Guard consisted of about eighty members of the Newport Artillery Company who were either disabled or of an advanced age that would prevent them from joining the First Rhode Island Regiment. The younger members of the company formed Company F of the First Rhode Island, which would take part in the Battle of Gettysburg, among other Civil War engagements. The Old Guard was commanded by Colonel William B. Swan, who had commanded the Artillery Company during the Dorr Rebellion in 1842.
51. The building that temporarily housed the Naval Academy still stands and is now an Elks Lodge.
52. Fort Adams Trust, "Historic Fort Adams Guided Tour Script."
53. Skomal, *Keeper of Lime Rock*.
54. Ibid., especially 92–99, 113.
55. Newport Mercury, "Fatal Accident."
56. The foregoing paragraphs on Ida Lewis are adapted from Troost-Cramer, *True Tales of Life and Death*, 49–51, 109 (notes 60–62).
57. Sherman was brevetted to the rank of major general, along with another officer of note, Henry Jackson Hunt, who had served as artillery commander of the Army of the Potomac.
58. The long delay in the granting of DuPont's medal was not unusual. Most of the Medals of Honor granted for heroism in the Civil War were awarded thirty years after the war's end.
59. The Zion Episcopal Church building underwent several incarnations, including as a vaudeville house, and is now the Jane Pickens Theatre on Washington Square.
60. All information on Miss Howard's shooting is taken from *Newport Daily News*, "Court-Martial at the Fort" and various articles, July 5–7 and 9, 1877; *Newport Mercury*, "Local Matters."

61. *Newport Mercury*, October 2, 1875.
62. *Newport Daily News*, "Noise of the Battle Afar," referring to the evening edition of the *Fall River Globe* for November 10 of the same year.
63. *Newport Mercury*, July 22, 1865.
64. Ibid., December 8, 1866.
65. Ibid., December 12, 1868.

Part III

66. This practice would regain popularity in the late twentieth century with the "one army" concept designed to diminish the distinctions between regular and reserve components of the armed forces.
67. These were designated the Sixth, Seventh and Eighth Provisional Coast Artillery Regiments.
68. This paragraph is adapted from Troost-Cramer, *True Tales of Life and Death*, 73–80. The quotation on Delia Geary's cause of death is from *Deaths Registered in the City of Newport, R.I.*
69. Wade, *Boston Globe*, September 3, 1956.
70. *Newport Daily News*, "To Provide Work for Unemployed Artists."
71. Ohio History Central, "Civil Works Administration."
72. This and the following seven paragraphs on Corporal Wilbraham are adapted from Troost-Cramer, *True Tales of Life and Death*, 69–71, 111–12 (notes 90 and 91).
73. *Newport Daily News*, July 24, 1941.
74. Adams, Letter to John Adams, March 31, 1776, Massachusetts Historical Society.
75. Titus and Foley, "Preservation Plan for the Military Cemetery at Fort Adams," 26.
76. The Henry family tragedy is adapted from Troost-Cramer, *True Tales of Life and Death*, 34–37.
77. The authors are indebted to Audrey Hopf for her kind permission to publish this photograph.
78. Constance A. Casey's reminiscences are taken entirely from the Fort Adams Oral History Project, July 29, 2003, conducted by Michael E. Bell.
79. Doris V. Shoesmith's reminiscences are taken entirely from the Fort Adams Oral History Project, July 22, 2003, conducted by Michael E. Bell.

80. Hamill siblings' and Mrs. Rondeau's reminiscences are taken from the Fort Adams Oral History Project, July 16, 2003, conducted by Michael E. Bell.
81. The chapel itself was nondenominational. Ms. Gilles recalled that each Sunday morning "Father would bring out everything you need for a Catholic Mass" and that the Catholic and Protestant congregations never even ran into each other while preparing for services.
82. Ms. Gilles's undated memoir is titled "Fort Adams Memoirs—1943/1944." It is unpublished and was discovered in the Fort Adams Trust archives by author Kathleen Troost-Cramer. Ms. Gilles also participated in the Oral History Project on July 16, 2003, and much of that interview (again with Michael E. Bell) is repeated in her memoir.

PART IV

83. Earle, Letter to the Newport Historical Society, August 23, 1956.
84. Ibid.
85. Ibid.
86. See Troost-Cramer, *True Tales of Life and Death*, 108 (note 43). Newport also boasted another "summer White House": Hammersmith Farm, home of Hugh Auchincloss, who married Janet Bouvier, mother of Jacqueline Bouvier. Jacqueline would marry John F. Kennedy in a ceremony at Newport's St. Mary's Church. (Coincidentally, Hammersmith's property abuts Fort Adams, and St. Mary's was built by the same Irish laborers who worked on Fort Adams in the 1840s.) The wedding reception was held at Hammersmith, and during his presidency, Kennedy summered at the estate. Hammersmith Farm was open for tours for several decades, but it is now privately owned and not accessible to the general public. Troost-Cramer, *True Tales of Life and Death*, 39, 60–61, 110 (note 74).
87. The Eisenhower House currently contains park offices and is not open to the public.
88. Fort Adams is still used as the venue for both the Jazz and Folk Festivals today, in addition to many other events throughout the season in the months from May to October.
89. See Troost-Cramer, *True Tales of Life and Death*, 21–29.

BIBLIOGRAPHY

The vast majority of this book is a reproduction of John T. Duchesneau's 2007 online work, "The History of Fort Adams: The Rock on Which the Storm Will Beat" (see reference information in the section titled "Websites and Online Databases" below). This work, the result of years of research by John, provides the foundation for the present volume, although some parts of that website have been rearranged, edited or cut for purposes of length and ease of reading in the format of a nonfiction print publication. The reader is therefore directed to John's online history for a fuller treatment of topics and sources employed.

This online work was transcribed as a kind of skeleton for the present volume, so a comparison of this book with the online history will show that the two are nearly identical in many places. It might even be said that this book is simply an expanded version of the website that John created out of the fruits of his own many years of research. Where material appearing on the website has been cut from the present volume, the sources for the cut material will not appear in the bibliography below. In many cases, that material appears instead in my book *True Tales of Life and Death at Fort Adams*, itself heavily indebted to John's research. Every effort has been made to include in this bibliography individual sources from John's online history where those are available.

Portions of *True Tales* also appear in this book where the accounts are pertinent to the periods and events discussed. The reader is referred to *True Tales* for a fuller discussion of topics and listing of sources used in that work.

BIBLIOGRAPHY

The section "WACs, Workers and Wives" contains entirely new research gained mostly from the Fort Adams Oral History Project.

–Kathleen Troost-Cramer

PRIMARY SOURCES

Adams, Henry. "Count Edward de Crillon." *American Historical Review* 1, no. 1 (October 1895): 51–69.

———. *History of the United States of America During the Administration of James Madison.* New York: Library of America, 1986.

American State Papers. Vol. 16. "Report of 1811."

Annual Military Reports, Rhode Island, 1883. Rhode Island: published by the adjutant general of Rhode Island, 1907. Available at the University of Rhode Island Library.

Bell, Michael E., comp. Fort Adams Oral History Project. Fort Adams, Newport, Rhode Island, July 2003.

Congressional Serial Set, No. 54, Section 98.

Cullum, George W. *Cullum's Biographical Register of Graduates of the United States Military Academy.* Cambridge, MA: Riverside Press, 1891.

———. *Cullum's Historical Sketch of the Defenses of Narragansett Bay.* Washington, D.C.: self-published, 1884.

Deaths Registered in the City of Newport, R.I., for the Year Ending December 31, 1918. Published in 1919.

Earle, Ralph, Jr. Letter to the Newport Historical Society, August 23, 1956. U.S. Naval Base, Office of the Commander, Newport, Rhode Island. NB31/Serial 1333. Provided by the Fort Adams Trust.

Gilles, Irene (Rena). "Memoir of Fort Adams—1944/1945." Unpublished manuscript discovered in the Fort Adams Trust archives by author Kathleen Troost-Cramer.

Newport Daily News. "Court-Martial at the Fort." July 13, 1877.

———. "The Noise of the Battle Afar." November 11, 1887.

———. "Soldiers Commended for Rescue Efforts." July 24, 1941.

———. "To Provide Work for Unemployed Artists: Fort Adams Building to be Decorated Under CWA." January 11, 1934.

BIBLIOGRAPHY

———. Various articles. September 14, 1853; July 5, 6, 7, 9, 13, 1877; September 16, 1906; June 14, 1910; July 8, 11, 1910; January 26, 27 and 28, 1925; June 20, 1925; June 11, 1942; August 11, 1943; March 29, 1946; April 14, 1947; September 12, 1956; July 25, 1960; September 5, 1972; December 15, 1978; December 4, 1998; May 22, 2001.
Newport Journal. Various articles. August 30, 1902; September 6, 13, 1902.
Newport Mercury. "Fatal Accident." October 22, 1842. Contained in research conducted by Father Robert Hayman at Providence College, Rhode Island, and given to the Fort Adams Trust by Vin Arnold.
———. "Fort Adams." July 17, 1886.
———. "Fort Adams Anniversary." May 27, 1922.
———. "Local Matters." July 7, 1877.
———. Various articles. July 9, 1799; July 5, 1817; October 21, 1826; June 22, 1833; July 22, 1836; April 30, 1842; July 30, 1842; August 6, 1842; January 21, 1843; September 11, 1843; May 31, 1845; July 5, 1845; August 23, 1845; September 20, 1845; May 30, 1846; October 3, 1846; May 29, 1847; July 10, 1847; September 17, 1859; January 5, 19, 1861; October 25, 1862; May 9, 1863; December 19, 1863; February 27, 1864; March 8, 1864; August 1, 20, 1864; May 10, 1865; July 22, 1865; November 11, 1865; March 10, 1866; June 9, 1866; December 8, 1866; July 4, 1868; December 12, 1868; June 12, 1869; September 25, 1869; June 28, 1870; September 27, 1870; October 2, 1875; August 11, 1877; August 26, 1882; March 17, 1907; May 11, 1907; June 29, 1907; April 18, 1947; September 2, 1949.
"An Old Resident." "Fort Adams in 1858–61: Its Neglected Condition Previous to the War of the Rebellion." *Newport Daily News,* July 26, 1901.
Providence Bulletin. Various articles. July 29, 1963; August 24, 1981.
Providence Journal. Various articles. July 24, 1941; May 28, 1950; June 15, 1951; May 22, 1965; July 30, 1972.
Report of the Secretary of War, 1802.
Stiles, Ezra. *The Literary Diary of Ezra Stiles.* Vols. 2.5 and 2.8. New York: Charles Scribner's Sons, 1901.
United States Military Reservations, etc. Office of the Judge Advocate General, United States Army. Washington, D.C.: Government Printing Office, 1916.
Wade, Harold. *Boston Globe,* September 3, 1956. Article referring to Fort Adams as the "country club of the army."

BIBLIOGRAPHY

SECONDARY SOURCES

American National Biography. Vol. 10. Article by Sylvia Larson. American Council of Learned Societies. New York: Oxford University Press, 1999, 611–13.

Catton, Bruce. *The American Heritage Picture History of the Civil War.* New York: American Heritage, 1982. Originally published in 1960.

Downs, Winfield Scott. *Encyclopedia of American Biography.* N.p.: American Historical Society, 1970.

Fort Adams Trust. "A Brief History of Restoration." Unpublished booklet, Newport, Rhode Island, 2011.

———. "Historic Fort Adams Guided Tour Script." Unpublished booklet, Newport, Rhode Island, 2011.

Gatchel, Theodore L. "The Rock on Which the Storm Will Beat: Fort Adams and the Defenses of Narragansett Bay." *Newport History* 67, no. 230 (1995): 1–35.

Johnson, Allen, and Dumas Malone, eds. *Dictionary of American Biography.* Vol. 4. American Council of Learned Societies. New York: Charles Scribner's Sons, 1996, 549–50.

McBurney, Christian M. *The Rhode Island Campaign: The First French and American Operation in the Revolutionary War.* Yardley, PA: Westholme, 2011.

1112th Area Service Unit (ASU). "History of Fort Adams." Unpublished booklet, 1952.

Robinson, Willard B. "Fort Adams: American Example of French Military Architecture." *Rhode Island History* 34, no. 3 (1975): 77–94. The Rhode Island Historical Society, Providence, Rhode Island.

Skomal, Lenore. *The Keeper of Lime Rock: The Remarkable True Story of Ida Lewis, America's Most Celebrated Lighthouse Keeper.* Philadelphia: Running Press, 2002.

Troost-Cramer, Kathleen. *True Tales of Life and Death at Fort Adams.* Charleston, SC: The History Press, 2013.

Wilson, James Grant, and John Fiske, *Appleton's Cyclopaedia of American Biography.* N.p.: D. Appleton, 1889.

BIBLIOGRAPHY

WEBSITES AND ONLINE DATABASES

Adams, Abigail. Letter to John Adams, March 31, 1776. Massachusetts Historical Society. www.masshist.org/publications/apde/portia.php?id=AFC01d244.
American State Papers. "Foreign Affairs," Vol. 3, 545–54. Library of Congress. http://www.loc.gov.
Artillery Company of Newport Homepage. www.newportartillery.org.
Coast Defense Study Group Database. cdsg.org.
Duchesneau, John T. "The History of Fort Adams: The Rock on Which the Storm Will Beat." www.oocities.org/~jmgould/adamshist.html.
Find a Grave. "Pierre Gustave Toutant Beauregard." Record added February 1, 1999. www.findagrave.com.
Hills, Waring. "Mount Pleasant Almost Starts 'The War.'" Patriots Point, South Carolina, 2014. http://www.patriotspoint.org/news_events/mount-pleasant-almost-starts-the-war.
"March 9 1812: Henry's Papers Delivered to Congress." 1812now.blogspot.com/2012/03/march-9-1812-henrys-papers-delivered-to.html.
Ohio History Central. "Civil Works Administration." www.ohiohistorycentral.org/w/Civil_Works_Administration?rec=863.
Titus, Daniel P., and Gerald Foley. "Preservation Plan for the Military Cemetery at Fort Adams." *Faculty and Staff—Articles & Papers*, no. 30 (2001). Digital Commons, Salve Regina University. http://digitalcommons.salve.edu/fac_staff_pub/30.
Wikimapia. "Perry Mill (1835)—Newport Bay Club & Hotel." http://wikimapia.org/21162073/Perry-Mill-1835-Newport-Bay-Club-Hotel.

INDEX

A

Adams, John Quincy, President 35
Allen, Maude 85, 88, 111
Almond, Lincoln, Governor (Rhode Island) 123
Anderson, Robert 44–47
anti-submarine net in Narragansett Bay 92, 103, 107
Army Corps of Engineers
  begins restoration on Fort Adams 119
Army of the Potomac 52
artists commissioned to create murals at Fort Adams 88, 90

B

Barnard, John G. 27
barracks fire (1947) 112, 113
Battle of Bull Run (First Manassas) 37, 47
Battle of Cedar Creek 60
Battle of Chapultepec 37, 47
Battle of Fredericksburg 52
Battle of Rhode Island 18
Battle of Spotsylvania 52
Beauregard, Pierre Gustave Toutant 28, 44–47

Bernard, Simon, Baron 25–27, 34
Best, Clermont 49
Bishop, Mary Richmond 50
British Royal Navy 16, 115
Brown, John Nicholas 112, 116
Burnside, Ambrose 37, 49–54
  governor (Rhode Island) 53
  state senator (Rhode Island) 54
Burnside Breech-loading Carbine 50
Burnside Expedition 51
Burnside's Bridge (Battle of Antietam) 51

C

cemetery, Fort Adams 59, 100
Citizens' Military Training Camps (CMTC) 88
Civil Works Administration (CWA) 90. *See* artists commissioned to create murals at Fort Adams
Connelly, Edwin 119
construction materials 32
countermines. *See* tunnels
Cullum, George W. 27
Cumberland Gap 52
Cushing, Henry, Brevet Major 75

Index

D

Davis, Harry C. 57
De Crillon, Edouard, Count 21–23
Downing, Antoinette 116
draft riots of July 1863 61
DuPont, E.I. 59, 60

E

Earle, Ralph, Jr., Rear Admiral
  expresses plans to demolish Fort Adams 114, 115
Eisenhower, Dwight D., President
  summers at Fort Adams 116
Endicott Period 69, 92, 156–162
Engineer Board 24

F

First System fortifications 18
Floyd, John, Secretary of War 50
Ford, Walter L. 57
Fort Adams
  becomes tourist attraction and event center 117
  "birth certificate" 29, 30
  deactivated 113
  declared Landmark at Risk 119
  designated National Historic Landmark 118, 119
  in disrepair post–Civil War 63, 66
  public protest saves fort from destruction 115
  rededicated as National Historic Landmark 123
  restoration work 124, 125
  soldiers awarded Soldier's Medal 90, 95
Fort Adams Foundation 117–120
  established 116
Fort Adams Trust 120, 124, 168
Fort Days 41
Fortifications Board 24
Fort Sumter 44–47
  bombardment of 45
  casualties 46
  surrender of 46

G

Gates, William, Colonel 41
Goat Island, fortifications 16
Grant, Ulysses S., General 53
Grimm, Selmer, Private
  court-martialed 63
  shoots Minnie Howard 62

H

Hale, Frank, Colonel 119, 123
Hathaway, William H. 57
Hector, Charles, Comte d'Estaing 17
Henry, John, Captain 20–23
Hill, A.P., General 49, 52
HMS *Liberty* 16
Howard, Minnie 61
  recovers 63
  shot 62
Howarth, George
  commandant of Fort Adams Foundation 117
Hurricane of 1938 92, 107

I

improvements to living quarters 67, 69
Irish
  establish Catholicism in Newport 32
  laborers at Fort Adams 30
  presence in Newport County 30

K

Kennedy, John Fitzgerald, President 32
Kennedy, Patrick, Representative 120

L

Lafayette, Marquis de 17
Lemnitzer, Lyman G., Lieutenant 88
Lewis, Ida 55–57, 59
  awarded Gold Lifesaving Medal, First Class 57

INDEX

fires shots to direct Fort Adams soldiers to safety 57
saves two Fort Adams soldiers 56, 57
Lincoln, Abraham, President 45, 50

M

MacGregor, Alexander 30, 32
Madison, James, President 21–23
Magruder, John B., Captain 41, 42
McCarthy, Edward B., Colonel 113
McClellan, George B., Major General 50, 52
mines installed in Narragansett Bay 92
mock battles 63
   as precursors to Joint Operations 63
   World War II 74
Monroe, James, President 24, 25, 29
Morgan's Raiders 52
Moulton, Thomas 57

N

Narragansett Bay Harbor Defenses (NBHD) 112
National Guard 67, 74, 75, 79, 85, 120, 123, 138, 163
Naval War College 114
Naval War College Museum exhibit at Fort Adams 125
navy housing, removed 119
Newport Artillery Company 16, 19, 47, 67, 119, 120, 123
Newport Folk Festival 117, 118
Newport Jazz Festival 117, 118

O

officers' quarters, Civil War era 49, 50

P

Paiva-Weed, Teresa, Senator 119
Palermo, Anthony, Colonel 120
Pastore, John O., Governor (Rhode Island) 112

Payne, Matthew M., Major 35
Pell, Claiborne, Senator 116, 120
Pierce, Benjamin K., Lieutenant Colonel 36, 130

Q

Quarters One ("Eisenhower House") 115, 116
Queen Anne's War 16

R

Ransom, Truman B., Colonel 36, 37, 48
recreational facilities between the world wars 85
Reed, Jack, Senator 120
Revolutionary War 16–18
Rhode Island, declares independence 16, 17
Rhode Island Historic Preservation Commission 116
Rochefontaine, Stephen, Major 18
Root, Elihu, Secretary of War 74

S

Schimmel, B.H., Major 113
sham attack. *See* mock battles
Sheehan, William 57, 59
Shepherd, Oliver L., Colonel 48
Sherman, Thomas W., Colonel 59, 132
Siege of Knoxville 52
Siege of Petersburg 52
Slocum, John S., Colonel 47
Smith, Mark Wentworth, Ordnance Sergeant 43, 44
Smith, Mary Beth 123
Southern Redoubt (at Fort Adams) 37–40
Spanish influenza 81
   impact on Fort Adams 81
Sprague, William S., Governor (Rhode Island) 47, 50
St. Mary's Church 32

INDEX

T

Talcott, Andrew, First Lieutenant
  first supervisor of construction 27
Taylor, Erich A. O'D., Senator 116, 119
Third System fortifications 27
Totten, Joseph G., Lieutenant Colonel
  27–30, 34, 35, 44
Tousard, Louis 19
tunnels 34

U

U-53 79
U-853 95, 99
Uhri, George, Sergeant 60
United Nations, plans for
  headquarters at Fort Adams
  112, 116
United States Naval Academy 47
United States Navy
  takes ownership of Fort Adams 114
  turns over Fort Adams to State of
    Rhode Island 116

W

Wade, Jennie 61
War of 1812 18, 23
west wall/west curtain, recreational
  facilities 72, 73
Wetmore, George Peabody, Senator
  discontinues service charges during
    summer months 76
Wilbraham, Walter K.
  car crash 95
  dies at fort hospital 95
  performs rescue at sea 93, 94
Women's Army Corps (WAC) 101

ABOUT THE AUTHORS

JOHN T. DUCHESNEAU is a resident of Newport, Rhode Island, and has worked, off and on, as a tour guide at Fort Adams since 1995. His interest in military history started in his childhood, and he has visited almost all of the coast defense forts in the northeastern United States, as well as a few in the South. He is a graduate of Rogers High School in Newport and holds a bachelor's degree from Rhode Island College and a master's degree in political science from the University of Rhode Island. He is a master sergeant in the Rhode Island National Guard and has served on four overseas deployments, including two tours in Iraq.

Photo by Matthew "Doc" Perry.

Aside from history, his interests include genealogy, travel and fine dining. He is active in numerous organizations, including the Artillery Company of Newport, the Military Order of the Loyal Legion of the

United States, the Rhode Island Society of the Sons of the Revolution, the Sons of Union Veterans, the Sons of the American Revolution, the Military Order of Foreign Wars, the Veterans of Foreign Wars and the American Legion. He is also an honorary member of the Providence Marine Corps of Artillery.

K ATHLEEN TROOST-CRAMER's first book, *True Tales of Life and Death at Fort Adams*, focusing on the real-life stories of the men and women who lost their lives at the fort, was published by The History Press in June 2013. Kathleen grew up in Portsmouth, Rhode Island, and developed a keen interest in local history at an early age. She went on to become a tour guide at several locations, including the Newport mansions, Belcourt Castle, Hammersmith Farm, the Lizzie Borden Bed & Breakfast/Museum in Fall River and, finally, Fort Adams. Visit Kathleen's website at www.ktroostc.wix.com/books.

www.ingramcontent.com/pod-product-compliance
Lightning Source LLC
Chambersburg PA
CBHW060758100426
42813CB00004B/867